SOCCER ZONES

SOCCER ZONES

WRITINGS OUT OF AMERICAN SOCCER

EDITED BY

Anne Harding Woodworth

WITH AN INTRODUCTION BY

George Vecsey

SPI

Soccer Prose, Inc.

Published 1994

Printed in the United States of America

Library of Congress Catalog Card Number: 93-86225
CIP Data available through the Library of Congress
ISBN 0-9638330-0-6

TO THE DEFENDERS IN MY LIFE

FLW

HGL

PAL

. . . Sprouting alike in broad zones and narrow zones.

—Walt Whitman, in "Leaves of Grass"

Contents

Preface

Soccer in the United States is and it isn't. It's catching on; it'll never catch on. It does and it doesn't. It's fast. It's slow. High score, low. Everybody knows no sport that doesn't use hands will ever catch on in America. Then we watch those incredible throw-ins.

"You are getting closer, America, to the roundball game," wrote Rob Hughes in the *International Herald Tribune* (March 10, 1993). Yet, didn't we show our soccer talent way back in World Cup 1950? We've been "getting closer" for so long. There's all this yes and no about American soccer.

That's how this book came about. Prose, poetry, and soccer. Are they compatible? Certainly not. Definitely, yes. Macho game. Gentle game. Men and women.

Defensive and offensive. Like the sweeper, that vociferous, pointing captain of the defense with the subtle eye for the occasional sudden move forward, this book reflects soccer in America today.

When you're from a city like Detroit, as I am, a sports-mad city, whose collective heart heaves with pride at the mere thought of having professional teams in all four big-time, big-paying sports—when you're from a city like that and you happen to think, perhaps even say, in a mumbling and quiet way, that soccer tops every team sport you know of in excitement, entertainment, subtlety, finesse, and—hold on now—beauty, you're risking any knowledgeability, credibility, and lucidity you might have established. "Good old Anne. She still has her sense of humor," say the unbelievers, who call an anthology of prose and poetry coming out of American soccer one of those ultimate oxymorons.

And this is where the paradox that is soccer in the U.S. just begins.

Because the truth of the matter is that an awful lot of people across the land, even in Detroit, happen to think soccer *is* tops.

This anthology is witness to parents who truly believe in their children as soccer players, sports writers who understand and appreciate soccer in America, writers who see soccer as a world language, poets who have felt the rhythms and cadences of the pitch, the American abroad, the foreigner in America.

The evolution of this book parallels that of soccer in America. When word got out that I was looking for prose and poetry on soccer for this anthology, parents, coaches, and players were the first to respond with manuscripts that were very touching, quickly making it clear that soccer strikes chords in the human spirit. That is why teams and leagues around the country have sprung up through the good work of caring parents and modest soccer fans, through people who laugh over soccer, and cry. Soccer has a lot to do with families in America: family dinners missed because of games, family outings denied, family trips not taken. "These are your children, America, and about to make you proud," wrote journalist Robert Markus in a program booklet for a U.S. Olympic qualifying match (May 10, 1992).

Soon professional writers began to respond, with letters of enthusiasm, with their ideas, and with their own stories to contribute to the anthology.

Still there were the skeptics. Sportsman, writer, editor and friend Thomas McGuane made an unusual comparison of soccer's striving in his Introduction to *The Best American Sportswriting 1992*, implying that it is somewhat akin to the old children's field-day relay race with an egg on a spoon. But there's always hope. When Tom heard about this anthology, he wrote to me, "I think you're doing a fine bit of consciousness-raising!" The consciousness is out there. This book is palpable evidence of it. You can hold soccer in your hands now, flip a page, and feel the spine.

And the paradox continues. Why so few professional teams in America? Why all the youth teams? Why the failures? Why the successes? Why the low salaries? Why the high ones? Why indoors? Why outdoors? Indoors on grass? Outdoors on artificial turf? Why no hands? And what about the small crowds? What about the huge ones? And where are the unruly ones? We've seen the crowds with flags and hot dogs and soft drinks, the wave, the "U - S - A" chant.

It's here. It's not here. It's here.

Here in America. And it's not like any other sport in this country. It's growing at its own pace and going in its own directions. It is innocence. It is experience. It's local, it's global; broad zones and narrow zones. Every size, age, and gender—which is why for everything you believe in American soccer, you'll find the opposite is also true, the complement, and the duplicate.

No hands, and much applause for soccer in America.

ANNE HARDING WOODWORTH

Acknowledgments

The encouragement to pursue the compilation of this book was very gratifying, beginning with an informal advisory group that included novelist and detective Paul Bishop; Dick Johnson of the Sports Museum of New England; and Charlie Shaw of Cranbrook Kingswood School. Frank Dell'Apa of the *Boston Globe* was also extremely helpful in introducing me to potential contributors. My husband, Fred Woodworth (Amherst #16), fell immediately, with all the natural grace in the world, into the soccer-ridden life my sons, Greg and Alexi Lalas, had shared with me for years. I am indebted to Bill Littlefield for his encouragement as well as for his editorial help on some of the manuscripts and to my old friend Dick Rosenbaum for his role in the design and production process.

AHW

SOCCER ZONES

Introduction

GEORGE VECSEY

Let me tell you about the day I made a bit of a fool of myself in the name of soccer. I was touring an ancient Roman settlement in Wales, and I wandered into an old amphitheatre, now mostly chunks of stone on grassy embankments.

As I walked across the lush green lawn, I felt myself in a soccer stadium. This is just the way my mind works, and I do not apologize. I had cushy walking shoes on, and I began jogging downfield, as it were, dribbling a soccer ball, which was real despite being invisible. Then I dished the ball off into the corner and dodged toward the goal, setting up one of those magnificent triangle plays that work just every so often. Bing-bing-bing! I leaped into the air and I took the return pass and I headed the ball into the opposite corner of the invisible goal. SCORE!

Unfortunately, an entire busload of Welsh schoolchildren had just entered the ancient amphitheatre, and they were watching me from twenty meters—a middle-aged man with a grey beard, leaping in the air, jerking his head forward. They did not cheer, but I would like to think some of them understood what I was about, because it is their game. It is everybody's game. Now it is even growing in North America, spread by the very same starry-eyed types who have contributed to this book.

I am one of those romantics, an American-born general sports

1

columnist for a major newspaper, the *New York Times*. I cover everything, but I am the rare American sports columnist who plots and plans his World Cup four years in advance, but goes to the Super Bowl only if there is some personal reason like seeing one of my children or being warm.

Most of my American colleagues my age bray about soccer's low scores. They absolutely do not get it, and never will. But an entire generation of sportswriter is coming along, men and women who have played the game, who have covered a World Cup, who have taken their children to soccer practice. In ten years, the tenor of American sportswriting will not be so glibly ignorant about the world's game.

The word is being passed on in books like this. These are love stories, written by men and women who recognize that kicking a soccer ball is one of the true pleasures in life. Soccer is a romantic notion in the United States, pursued by dreamy idealists who realize they have found something special. They write poems to soccer, they write short stories to soccer, they leave home to play soccer.

The United States has its current "Lost Generation," just the way the youth of the twenties followed Hemingway and Fitzgerald and Stein to Europe, seeking an older, wiser way of doing things. This generation is perhaps not so much lost but strayed. We know where they are. They are playing soccer in Western Europe, Eastern Europe, the Middle East and Latin America. They do it for money, to some degree, and surely they do it for the experience of playing against the best competition. But mostly they leave home for the reason youths have always left home. For love.

In our modern-day love stories, the Lost Generation plays for scrubby fifth-division clubs in rural France, for impoverished second-division teams in the economic chaos of a former Communist country. Some of them make it to the top in a distant land, like John Harkes who has played in cup games in Wembley, the spiritual home of English soccer. John Harkes has acquired an English accent. No, not an English accent, the British tell me, but a Sheffield accent. It blends with his New Jersey accent when he comes home to play with the U.S. National Team. He is a tough guy and a very professional midfielder, but even in the acquired accent I detect the romanticism of a young man who has found something. He left home to become a footballer.

This may sound jaded or narrow on my part, but I think all the joys of playing pickup games with strangers, the inner thrill of dribbling a ball in an empty playground, so lovingly detailed in this book, stem from the existence of the great leagues, the championships, the cup games in the biggest cities in the world.

And not just for men. The eleven-year-old daughter of friends had just been to a 2–0 victory by Brazil over the United States in Connecticut. Carrie acknowledged that the American men were not so great that day, but she added, "The women are the champions." And that is true. American women have a loftier image than the men. They can play their private soccer game with the memory of the American women capturing the first world championship in China in 1991.

This is new for Americans. Self-consciously we dream about scoring the big goal. It is not that way for the Hispanic men in my town. I see them in the evening when I go for my jog at the high-school track. There are fifteen or twenty of them, training hard together, a soccer team of men from El Salvador and Colombia and Honduras and Guatemala. They do not seem romantic or self-conscious, because this is their game, from the time they were born. They will not be surprised next weekend, in their game against some other "ethnic" team, if somebody yanks their hair, or elbows them in the windpipe, or even grabs them in a very private area, the way the dreaded defender, Vinny Jones of Wimbledon, has been known to do. They know soccer can be as brutal as a kick in the ankle, just like life.

These men are not dreamers. They already know that soccer will not be a way out of anything for them, but they practice the game because it is theirs in some deep, understood fashion. But also in my town, little children diligently dribble a soccer ball

4

around a pink rubber cone, learning rudimentary skills, the way Diego Armando Maradona learned his skills kicking a ragball in a dirty alley in a hard-bitten quarter of Buenos Aires. For them, soccer is a game, played on leafy fields, with parents waiting on park benches, their Volvos and Hondas parked nearby. And some of them will one day learn the connection to the desperate world of Vinny Jones and Diego Armando Maradona. They will have their introduction to real soccer.

Every soccer romantic in this book and elsewhere can tell you about The First Time. I was fortunate enough to have two First Times—one as a player of sorts, one as a soccer correspondent of sorts.

My introduction to soccer happened at Jamaica High School, in the borough of Queens, in the city of New York, in the fall of 1954. We didn't have American football, so somebody talked me into going out for soccer. Our coach was a little old gym teacher making five hundred dollars extra, and his job was to open the ball bag and dump the balls on the hardscrabble field. We learned most of our soccer from our star player, a German-American guy who played center forward sometimes, and goalie sometimes, and polished his game in an ethnic league on weekends.

I can remember my teammates: Greek, Swedish, French, Swiss, German, Italian, Puerto Rican, Venezuelan, half a dozen American-born guys. We played six different styles. I was a fullback. What a joke. I can remember hearing Hispanic players coming down the field at us shouting "Arriba! Arriba!" But mostly I can remember a guy named Bubbi who played for Grover Cleveland High School, making moves around me that I could neither see nor believe, and blasting the ball past our innocent goalie. I had more chance of playing for the Brooklyn Dodgers than stopping Bubbi.

That was my introduction to playing soccer. Twenty-eight years later I finagled a trip to the World Cup in Spain, and found myself in a press section, which was, amazingly, only ten rows up from the field in a homey little stadium called Sarria in the city of Barcelona. There I could see an Italian defender named Claudio Gentile raking his cleats on the shins of Diego Armando Maradona. Thunk! I could hear the impact of Gentile's boots on the hard flesh and bone of Diego Armando. Why hadn't I thought of that when I was in high school? Occasionally, the lone official would whistle at Gentile and call a foul on him, but how in the world could you call everything?

Then all of a sudden, bing-bing-bing, the ball moved in triangular fashion up the field, so fast I could not follow it. It was like trying to mark Bubbi all over again. Suddenly the ball was in the net, and I had not seen the sequence. I turned to the reporter next to me, an American-Italian guy with the Associated Press in Rome, named Enrico Jacomini.

"What happened?" I asked.

"Graziani to Cabrini to Rossi down the left side," he said, or words to that effect. I realized you had to note every man who touched the ball because you never know. In soccer, you just never know. I think that is why I love the game so much. This is why I sit in front of my television set in New York every Sunday morning, religiously, as I like to say, watching the Italian league games, live from Italy. I sit in my den and I wish I were in Genoa or Torino or Milano. I dream. A lot of us dream. We are romantics.

PART I

GLOBAL CONNECTIONS

"Who Are You? And What's That Game You're Playing?"

BILL LITTLEFIELD

I don't know a lot about soccer—a condition that will become more and more apparent as this story lopes along—but I don't kow a lot about darts, either, or chess, or the luge, and I've written about all of *them*. I figured I'd make up for the absense of expertise with enthusiasm and the willingness to be where the story was, even before it was there. That's why I was standing on the edge of the Foxboro Stadium field when the U.S. team came off it last Tuesday after the final practice before it beat the English team and Great Britain collapsed into self-loathing.

But one thing at a time. I recognized nobody among the players coming off the practice field, of course. I picked one at random and asked him a few questions. In a faint English accent he expressed confidence in his team and faith that soccer would catch on in this country. These were not revolutionary sentiments, but they were serviceable, certainly. When we'd finished talking, I asked the young man his name. For a beat and a half he looked at me incredulously. Then he said, "John Harkes."

I learned later that Harkes is one of the few U.S.-born players who has reached the top rank of competition overseas. He's a star for the delightfully named Sheffield Wednesday Club in the English League, and he was the first U.S. player to compete in

England's Football Association Cup Final. My asking him his name was roughly equivalent to an English interviewer making the same inquiry of Michael Jordan . . . or at least John Harkes looked at me as if he felt that way.

My theory is that that's why Harkes and his teammates beat the English team the next evening. They were mad at me. Anyway, the unexpected 2–0 win was a very large deal in England. The more rational tabloids called for the coach's resignation. The others wanted him executed. I know this because the day after the game, I got my first phone call ever from the BBC. A man in Bristol wanted to know if the Americans were dancing in the street. I looked out the window. "Not right now," I said.

"Well," he said, "we have the headlines from the Boston paper. It says, 'Blimey! U.S. Boots the Brits!' It says, 'All's Not Jolly For England!'"

"Right," I said. "But the headline that says 'Look Out Below— Red Sox Fall Under .500' is bigger."

The man in Bristol was undeterred. "Still," he said, "it must have been something. Was everyone packed into the pubs, watching the game on the telly?"

"A lot of people were watching the National Hockey League Finals," I said. "And the NBA Championship's final round. The soccer game wasn't on."

"What about hooligans?" the man from Bristol asked.

"I don't know what they were watching," I said.

That may have been where he gave up on the interview, because there was a pause, like the one that came after I asked John Harkes his name. Probably there was a producer giving the man in Bristol the cut sign through the wall of a glass booth. Or maybe he was holding up one finger to signify that the man in Bristol should lob the yank lout one more question, then bail out.

"Well, what about you?" the man in Bristol asked, and he didn't have to actually say, "you nit!" "What's this game going to mean to you?"

"I'll keep an open mind," I said, trying to be helpful. "I'll go to the video store and rent 'One Hundred Greatest Soccer Goals.' I mean Football . . . Football Goals, right?"

There was no answer, so I said, "football . . . football, right?" a couple more times before I realized the line was dead.

Hasta Luego, Ronald Reagan

Bryan J. Burkert

La Concha Playa, the largest beach in San Sebastian, is sparsely populated on another sun-drenched day. Behind me sits a concrete pier, anchoring a boardwalk that lines a half-mile of the ridge overlooking the strand. Seaweed, sea rot and beach trash line its cracked frame. The tide, rhythmically pitching against a backdrop of jagged cliffs and rumbling sea, rolls out. Siesta comes in.

Minutes later, the lethargy is broken as a swarm of whooping schoolboys hurl themselves upon the boardwalk and rush to claim a section of the freshly washed shoreline. Shirts, shoes and socks are anxiously discarded. A few splash into the foaming surf.

One boy stands firm, crosses his ankles and waits. Moments later another steps in behind. The boy with his ankles crossed leans back and yields his weight into his friend's waiting arms. As he is dragged, his path, carved in the moist sand by heavy feet, is clearly marked by the small trench he forges. Forty-some meters across, two other youths repeat the same process on a parallel plane. Once the sidelines are marked and shirts are positioned as goalposts, sides are quickly chosen, and positions are randomly set.

The tallest boy, his young body and his short black hair already glistening with sweat, yells, "¡Vamos! ¡Vamos!" He nudges the *pelota* forward with his left foot and the daily game begins once again.

*   *   *

San Sebastian, located on Spain's northern Atlantic coast, is twenty minutes from France and centuries removed from the country that claims it. The Basques, who populate this region, speak their own language, have their own culture, and reject Spanish sovereignty. They are fiercely independent; resent foreigners and occasionally use terrorism to highlight their struggle for separation. They possess a rogue passion; a unique blend of instinctive ferocity and beauty. On any manic evening they may celebrate and parade in the streets or swell with uproar and riot—torching a government building in protest.

The lone constant in Basque country, the only consistency I observed, is their unabashed love for the game they call *fútbol*. It not only unites their people, but also provides a singular bond with the rest of Spain. Among a population eager to resent me, I found the game a passport into their world.

My evenings, which I spent in San Sebastian's La Parte Vieja enjoying *calamari* and *cervezas*, were enjoyable but dulled with precious little company. My attempts to converse with the Basques were generally met with subtle, disheartening indignation. Amongst abject glares, disengaged dialogues and persistent indifference, I felt truly foreign.

My days I also passively passed, observing, yet not participating in, the afternoon *fútbol* matches. The young Basques were remarkable to watch.

Their game has both fire and grace. It moves with an erratic, chaotic flow tempered by a natural rhythm. Endless series of short, crisp passes and movement are punctuated by bursts of incredible individual aggressiveness and creativity. They play with a style that is pure. It is one of instinct.

If a European basketball fan came to America and stopped at a city park to observe a pickup game, he would have the same perception. Nothing seems coached or contrived. It's just youth who seemingly effortlessly demonstrate the beauty of a sport: juveniles who don't simply play a game, but live it.

As fascinated as I was with the characteristics of the daily match, as much as I ached to join them, each day as low tide came and the boys arrived, I was paralyzed by feelings of intrusiveness. It wasn't until fate interjected, on the second to last day of my stay, that I finally summoned the nerve to approach them.

This day, as the field was marked and sides were being chosen, I noticed that there was an uneven number. There were seventeen of them. My stomach knotted, and I moved closer to the field, anxious to play. I swallowed hard—dejection hit—as one boy headed for the sidelines; eight a side, one substitute. Disappointed I watched the game begin.

Soon I was working out in my head how to ask to play. I just couldn't wait any longer. "Quiero jugar contigo. ¿Es posible?" I thought.

As I rehearsed my lines, ready to assert myself, the boy on the sideline caught my eye and motioned for me to come over. My heart leapt. I tried not to seem too eager, so I slowly jogged over, restraining instincts to sprint.

"¿Quieres jugar?" he asked me.

"Sí, gracias, gracias," I quickly replied.

His thin young face broke into a smile. "¿Americano, no?"

"Sí, yo soy americano."

"Soccer!" he yelled and laughed. Then he called to the others on the field to tell them I would be playing and that I was an American. This was received with amusement. They shook their heads and stared at me like I was some oddity that would provide a diversion but little else. I think they expected me to pick up the ball and throw it.

One of the players, moving his stocky body with the arrogance of youth, came over and introduced himself to me as Aeor. In a combination of broken English and Spanish he instructed me to play on the right side. I tossed off my shirt and trotted over into position.

After ten minutes of exercising my right to run up and down

the field and little else, I snagged the ball from an opposing player who was rushing towards my goal and passed it back to my keeper.

Play resumed when my goalie inbounded the ball on the left sideline. Then, with a quick series of short passes and slashing, overlapping cuts, my left wing and left midfielder worked the ball deep into the opposition's end. Here, the wing dribbled the ball into the corner and before the charging defender could tackle, he smoothly stepped on the ball—deadened its spin— and heeled it back to the trailing midfielder. Fluidly, with precise timing, the middie punched his bare left foot through the pass.

As the cross floated towards the front of the goal's right corner, I felt my pulsing muscles tense. A panting, pressing defender leaned into me. Instinctively, feeding some elbow into his gut, I turned and with a gasp and a muffled thump the descending *pelota* settled off my chest.

As it struck the packed sand, pivoting, I dropped the *pelota* back to the approaching Aeor. In perfect symmetry, not breaking stride, he fired a low, hard shot that skipped off the beach and sailed inches wide to the left.

Sweat-soaked and winded, I ran back into position. Aeor, glanced over at me, faintly nodded and turned away.

That was it. From then on it was magical. After that, exactly what I wanted to happen did. I began to fit in. Basically, the best way to describe it is, they let me play. The rhythm of the game I had admired for days I became part of.

I received passes so deftly struck that they often caught me off guard. It was simple. When I was open, the ball was passed to me. When I needed help, I was given support. And when I felt like being creative, I was given space. It was effortless to be part of their team.

For those hours—chasing a worn *pelota*, responding within the game's flow, working towards a simple, common goal, exchanging knowing glances and feeling part of a whole—I was just another boy playing *fútbol* at La Concha Playa. Cultural differences were nullified and familiarity came naturally.

16

As the tide swelled and the game ended, I introduced myself to some of the players. Combining my remedial Spanish with the few English phrases they knew we exchanged some shallow ideas. The conversation, overwhelmed with salutations, was hopelessly trivial. Minus the *pelota* and the harmony of play our cohesiveness languished.

As I slipped on my shirt and prepared to go, Aeor walked by and asked me if I wanted to play tomorrow.

"Sí, me gusta jugar mañana," I said.

Grinning sheepishly, he said, "Bueno. Hasta luego, Ronald Reagan." The others laughed and repeated "Ronald Reagan" to themselves, wishing they had thought of it. Then they all delivered their goodbyes, smirkingly calling me Ronald Reagan, as I said, "Hasta mañana," to them.

A Day in Trinidad

Roscoe Nance

Sunday, November 19, 1989. That's the day I came to understand what soccer is really about.

I thought I was up on the game. I had watched countless matches and had come to appreciate its beauty and athleticism; I had read about the hooliganism and violence that many associate with the game.

I discovered that day, when the U.S. national team played Trinidad & Tobago in Port-of-Spain, Trinidad, with a World Cup berth in the balance, that soccer also produces a passion among fans not equalled in any other sport.

The atmosphere was electric. Everything on the island came to a stop. For ninety minutes, the only thing in the world that mattered was on that pitch.

I had covered big-time college football games—Alabama vs. Auburn, Texas vs. Oklahoma, Georgia Tech vs. Georgia, and several bowl games—pro football and basketball and the Final Four. But the excitement they generated pales in comparison with what unfolded that day.

An entire nation lived and died with each pass and errant shot.

Kickoff was at 1 p.m., but the stadium was packed at 10 a.m. So you think the Orange Bowl halftime shows are a spectacle?

The pre-game festivities this day made them look like a side show. Countless steel bands and singers paraded around the stadium track whipping 35,000 red-clad spectators into a frenzy in anticipation of Trinidad earning its first World Cup berth. By the time the game began, they were spent.

One of the great tragedies of American soccer is that this game wasn't televised in the USA. If America could have seen the festive crowd and the high drama the game produced, there's no telling how many converts would have been won over.

Monday had already been declared a national holiday in anticipation of a victory by the home team on Sunday. When the U.S. won 1–0 on Paul Caligiuri's improbable goal from 35 yards to secure its first World Cup berth since 1950, the setting was perfect for trouble.

It wasn't difficult to envision a disappointed and angry crowd running amok. It never happened.

The Trinidadians partied their disappointment away. It was their way of acknowledging that the better team had won and saluting their team's effort. That's the way it should be, a festive celebration, not the ugliness that comes to many Americans' minds when they think of soccer.

That's the way it was the entire weekend. The Trinidadians wanted their team to win and would have done anything for a victory. But their support never went beyond the bounds of decency. They were good-natured in their verbal exchanges with American supporters, not mean-spirited and foul.

They were more than gracious hosts. Two of them, Ian and Steve—relatives of a co-worker of mine, went out of their way to make me feel at home.

Like so many other times when I've gone on assignments, I was given the phone number of someone to look up. Despite a few reservations, I called them late Saturday morning, and they offered to stop by my hotel for a chat. After they arrived, we talked incessantly about everything from American football—a game that made absolutely no sense to them—to Ian's striking resemblance to his cousin, my co-worker. They even offered to drive me to the stadium so I could pick up my credentials to cover the game.

A bustling crowd that could be expected on game day greeted us. Vendors were hawking their wares and stadium personnel were readying the pitch. After I was credentialed, I bought Ian and Steve each one of the "Road to Italy" T-shirts that were so popular among Trinidad supporters. They were blown away.

They then showed me around the island as we drank a few beers and talked. I saw Ian again Sunday morning outside the stadium. Even though he had a ticket, he wasn't certain if he would be allowed in. The stadium was already packed and fans were being turned back.

It was mind-boggling how a sporting event could so galvanize a nation. It began with thousands of chanting fans showing up to meet the U.S. team at the airport on Friday night and went on well into the wee hours of Monday morning. Everywhere you turned—the hotel lobby, the market, the radio—the only topic of conversation was Sunday's game. It was unreal.

It's not uncommon for some college towns to be engulfed in this same sort of mania during football season. But this was different. But then soccer is different. It's different because it's more than a sport. It's a way of communication; it's a way of bringing people together; it's an experience.

Some call it chess on grass. Others know it simply as football. But this day I discovered it's a game that touches people's very souls.

Ekecheiria Revisited

FRED L. WOODWORTH

Start with a middle-aged lawyer who loves the Olympic Games and sometimes even has Walter Mitty-ish fantasies of climbing the victory stand in some far-off, cosmopolitan place. Through molecular cross-blending, combine that person with a frustrated would-be classicist whose favorite course in college was "Four Greek Sites," one of the most obscure and least selected in the whole academic catalogue. What do you get? A person with a lemming-like drive to visit the sacred classical Greek site of Olympia in the western Peloponnesos, where the ancient games began in 776 B.C. This driven person was I in the fall of 1985.

Of all the beautiful, serene classical sites one can visit, Olympia is among the most peaceful and inspirational in impact. True, the topography of the place itself contributes greatly; the sacred Olympic grove is nestled between two lovely little rivers, the Alpheios and the Kladeos. The surrounding farming countryside is lush and green; the ruins themselves cover a large area, but are orderly and understandable. There is an elegant softness to them. You can actually enter the remains of the original Olympic stadium through the very same *krypte* (tunnel) used by the Olympic athletes of old.

Early on a cool, sunny October morning in 1985, I had the chance to jog several laps on the ancient course with two Soviet

20

men. While we couldn't converse in words, there were warmth and unspoken communication between us. I wonder what country they identify with now.

People of all nationalities walk, run, and just sit together in the sunny and shady ruins at Olympia. They hope and dream for a better day, when distinctions of mere nationality can be put aside and humankind will become more united in goals of peace, world-wide health, justice, tolerance, unselfishness and protection of the planet. These universal feelings are especially powerful and palpable at the mother of Olympic sites. They are in part traceable to *ekecheiria*, a formal truce or suspension of hostilities, which was declared among the constantly warring ancient Greek city-states. The Olympic truce enabled Greek athletes to travel safely to Olympia, compete and commune together, and return home without conflict. *Ekecheiria* involved the temporary putting aside of apparent or superficial differences for the purpose of realizing and expressing more basic points of human unity and similarity.

It is in these primal concepts and desires that one can explain the tourist's fascination with the ancient Olympic site, as well as our love of the modern Olympic games. Since the founding of the modern games in 1896 by Baron de Coubertin, the Olympic flame has been transported by torch every four years (global conflicts permitting) from the original Greek ruins to the city selected to hold the modern games. On the evening of July 25, 1992 the Olympic flame of this XXV Olympiad entered Montjuic Stadium in downtown Barcelona, Spain.

Fulfilling a dream to attend some Olympic competition somewhere during my lifetime, I also arrived in Barcelona on the evening of July 25th. I was there to see soccer, because by some magic—or plainly lucky—quirk of fate, I had fairly recently become the stepfather of a member of the soccer team. The U.S. Olympic Soccer Team was one of sixteen under-23 national teams that qualified for the final round of competition in Barcelona. Just getting there was a major accomplishment. The team was grouped in a round-robin first round with Italy, Kuwait, and Poland. Only two of these four teams would go on to the quarterfinals. While hopes were high, it was the consensus that our Group A might represent the toughest competition. Both Italy and Poland were rated as extremely strong. Kuwait was a question mark. The first match against Italy actually occurred the day before the opening ceremonies. Playing well in the second half, the U.S. lost to Italy 2–1. Our team was racked by injuries. Four or five starters were out. Nevertheless, the team showed that it could perform well against top world-class competition.

The remaining first-round games against Kuwait and Poland were to be played in Zaragoza, a fascinating ancient-and-modern town about 300 kilometers west of Barcelona, on the banks of the River Ebro. Except for the river valleys, this part of Spain is dry and starkly beautiful, sometimes even a desert. Throughout history, Zaragoza has been a key military and cultural crossroads. There are Roman ruins side-by-side with ornate Christian cathedrals and mysterious Moorish castles. Since Zaragoza was an Olympic venue only for soccer, there was no overcrowding, freneticism or Olympic hype. The soccer players, families and fans of the several national teams were welcomed warmly, but matter-of-factly. After all, soccer is a regular part of Spanish life.

Zaragoza's soccer stadium was a perfect jewel. Of medium size, the stadium's seating sections were alternately bright blue and white; the field below was a brilliant green. Games were played in the early evening to minimize the oppressive heat. On July 27th, the team defeated Kuwait 3–1, playing very sharply, especially in the second half. Again, injuries kept several players from playing. After the game, the Kuwaiti players and fans cheered the USA and held up signs thanking the U.S. for saving their country. It was quite a moment.

Finally the determining game against Poland became a reality on Wednesday, July 29th. Poland thus far was undefeated and not scored upon. The day passed very slowly. Players waited nervously in their hotel rooms. The game began at 7:00 p.m. sharp. Poland in pure white and the U.S. men in bright red. Both teams played their hearts out. After ninety minutes of surging and counter-surging, tough physical contact, and just plain excellent soccer, the score stood 2–2.

The whole U.S. team played well. I really don't know which team was better. Dusk was descending rapidly and the lights were on when the last whistle blew. The players from Poland and the U.S. embraced one another, exchanged game shirts and sat together for a time on the stadium floor. Because of the tie score, we knew that Poland would definitely move on at least to the quarterfinals and that the U.S. would almost certainly be eliminated. The U.S. fans were quiet and pensive.

At that moment, a small scene from the great movie *Glory* flashed into my head. You may recall it. The soldiers of the 54th Massachusetts had just had their first taste of the bitter, bloody combat of the Civil War. They had done well and fought bravely. Many battles still lay ahead. The commanding officer, speaking proudly of his hitherto untested troops said, "You should have seen them. They were a sight to see."

And you should have seen our U.S. Olympic Soccer Team in Spain. They were a sight to see. Soccer is the world's game, and our team played right up to world standards. We can all be proud.

For the players, coaches and families, life goes on. We wend our way back to our own lives, our own versions of reality, and to the future. If the ghost of Baron de Coubertin could have visited Zaragoza during the last week of July 1992, he would have approved of what he saw.

From my personal perspective, the Olympic spirit seems intact. You can draw a straight line from the ancient Greek concept of *ekecheiria* to the communication and competition among the nations at the Barcelona games.

Looking Back:
Soccer and America

SAM FOULDS

As a teenager, I lived in a neighborhood mostly of second-generation immigrants of the Dorchester section of Boston. Immigrants have played a vital role in American soccer.

My neighborhood was fast becoming an area of two- and three-decker houses, interspersed between the individual homes of old-time residents. Maybe because families were larger then and middle-class working folks lived in compact areas, our sports were localized. Our mode of transportation was either electric street car, foot or bike. There were no youth soccer leagues, no clinics, no summer camps. Our parents seldom concerned themselves with our sports or our sports aspirations, although the occasional father, uncle, older brother, or errant bystander, who may have played soccer in some place far away, would join in our fun.

My father was an immigrant from England, who, in spite of a love for baseball and the Red Sox, followed soccer religiously. Those of us neighborhood kids born on the U.S. side of the Atlantic during the early days of this century learned to play soccer in much the same way our peers overseas did; that is, on spare lots near home. Our games were played between pickup teams of indeterminate numbers and ages.

Before I went to high school, we had scrub games with maybe four or five players on a team, and two caps on the ground defined each goal. There was a fenced-in schoolyard, two sides of which were brick walls. That's where we usually played, waiting till the janitor went home in the afternoon so that we could enter the locked yard by some rather unconventional means. We used the walls in our games, sort of the way it's done in indoor soccer. Ordinary, everyday clothes and shoes were our uniforms, and the ball was more often than not a medium-sized heavy rubber beach ball, a tennis ball, or an old soccer-ball casing stuffed with newspaper.

I never had a coach, except for my father, or played with a full eleven until my teenage years at school, between 1918 and 1924. My coach was a math teacher, who read the rulebook as he went. Sometimes he would put as many as twenty on each side.

There was a boy from Holland on my team who knew the game, and as he and I passed the ball back and forth between us, thirty-six other players converged upon us to our chagrin. That Dutch boy was just one of many immigrants I knew, whose language of soccer I could speak, as I was growing up. For me it was an automatic way of communicating. And it worked both ways.

The Statue of Liberty and American soccer share a sense of history with each other. To many immigrants who have reached these shores, the Statue of Liberty has been a symbol of a new and productive future, and soccer has often been a comfortable vehicle by which they have found congeniality in their new country.

There's a lot of dialogue about the beginnings of American soccer. In 1862, the Oneida Football Club of Boston was formed by Gerritt Smith Miller of Peterboro, New York, who was a student at the Epes Sargent Dixwell Private Latin School of Boston. The club operated for three undefeated seasons; in fact not one goal was scored against them. The Oneidas played to an unwritten set of rules, which primarily called for a kicking game but which under certain circumstances allowed running with the ball. This caused some to say that the game was closer to the code of latter-day rugby than soccer.

The original rules for association football (soccer), which also allowed for carrying the ball under certain restrictions, were first promulgated in 1863 at London, England, and closely resembled the Oneida code, except that the Oneidas did not use goal posts. Actually, both soccer and rugby-type-football adherents convened at the London meeting. However, the rugby followers withdrew from the conference, when an anti-hacking resolution was incorporated into the rules, and eventually in 1871 they established their own rugby association.

Soccer became an intercollegiate sport on November 6, 1869 in a game between Princeton and Rutgers in New Brunswick, New Jersey. In 1876, however, rugby rules were adopted in colleges, and soccer lay dormant until 1881, when soccer-oriented newcomers from Britain and Ireland initiated a game with a group of native-born St. Louis players on the site of the present-day Busch Stadium. It heralded the revitalization of American soccer, and the game began to re-assert itself on American playing fields. It continued to do so for the next fifty years, during which more than 27 1/2 million immigrants entered the United States. If they were soccer players at any level, they had a pretty good vehicle for easing into the life stream of their new nation.

And it is these immigrants, both players and managers, who gave stability to soccer and ensured its continuance in America, so that American soccer is self-sustaining now as never before. It is the very multi-national character of soccer's beginnings, as well as the continued multi-cultural involvement in the game, that enhances soccer's all-American status.

Rediscovering the World Game

Dick Johnson

> To say that these men paid their shillings to watch the twenty two hirelings kick a ball is merely to say that a violin is wood and catgut, that Hamlet is so much paper and ink. For a shilling the Bruddersford AFC offered you Conflict and Art . . .
>
> J. B. Priestley, *The Good Companions*, c. 1929

As curator of The Sports Museum of New England, I toil as a sort of professional fan/spectator. Working at such a job in Boston has been one of the great privileges of my life. A chef should be so lucky to work in Paris, a writer in Ireland, or a climber in Nepal. Long before I attained this career status, I became a fan of all sports through the exploits of local heroes, such as the "Impossible Dream" 1967 Red Sox, Bob Cousy; Bill Russell; Bobby Orr; Gino Cappelletti; Jack "The Shot" Foley; and the many others who made their names in the finest all-around sports region in America.

Sometimes I feel a bit weary with the present state of sports in America, and I find myself caring just a little bit less about my teams. No doubt the proliferation of megabuck contracts and egos to match have soured me on much of what I once loved as a fan.

I was in just such a frame of mind in December of 1989 when an old sporting flame was rekindled in me during a discussion with my buddy Mike LaVigne regarding the inclusion of soccer within the then soon-to-be-built Sports Museum of New England. I found myself talking about teams and players I hadn't contemplated for nearly twenty years. As our discussion continued, it became clear that the exotic appeal of the game had never left me. Not only had I found an old friend, but I had also rediscovered the joy of sports through the vehicle of the world game. Once more the game on the field would take precedence over the board room and contract table. With the enthusiasm of a twelve-year-old, I would delve afresh into the history and tradition of a sport with roots in the land of my ancestors, a game unlike any other in its ability to inspire and entertain.

Little did I know the totality with which I would be reacquainted with the world game. In subtle and then more obvious ways, a sport escalates from being a mere pastime to becoming a way of life. So it was with soccer and me upon my rediscovery of the game. I bought a shortwave radio to pick up the BBC World Service for their Saturday morning "SportsWorld" program, a three-hour smorgasbord of soccer from across Britain. Not only is this program the perfect complement to a hearty English breakfast of tea, eggs, marmalade, and toast, but I still find myself in a state of wonder as I am transported to every game of Britain's sacred Saturday ritual and goals are scored—from Parkhead in Glasgow to the Plainmoor Ground at Torquay. There are ninety-two league teams in England situated in a land mass roughly the equivalent of the State of Alabama, and thirty-eight more in South-Carolina-sized Scotland. Amazing.

The Game Itself

> Football is the opera of the people.
>
> Stafford Heginbotham
> Chairman, Bradford City Football Club, c. 1985

In many ways the game of soccer is comparable to abstract painting. In order to truly appreciate the meaning, mystery, and magic of a canvas by an artist such as Mark Rothko, it helps one to have actually tried to make a painting. Just as many of the critics who dismissed Rothko never took up the brush, so too most critics of soccer have never attempted ninety minutes of spirited physical dialogue with a checkered ball and ten teammates.

It has been two decades since I attempted my first oil painting, and I still find myself planning vacations and daytrips in order to seek Rothkos in various galleries and museums. Similarly I find it difficult, if not impossible, to pass by a group of kids kicking a ball about without pausing to watch or asking to join in. In many ways they are painting their own abstract canvas, replacing color, form, and texture with passes, kicks, and headers, all in a swirling creation conveyed in the *lingua franca* that is soccer. And unlike in the analysis of a Rothko, no critics or interpreters are needed.

Instead of visiting Maine Road, Parkhead, Old Trafford and the San Siro to view the soccer equivalent of a gallery full of my favorite artists (by financial necessity, not choice!), I have attempted and succeeded at a task deemed impossible for most American adults, namely to program my VCR. Contrary to the Springsteen lyric that says of cable TV there are "fifty-seven channels and nothing's on," I have found my cable box to offer a bounty of soccer from full matches in English and Spanish to weekly highlight programs chronicling the English Premier League and Continental action.

I also figure that I am one of a handful of fanatics who haunt the world-renowned Out of Town newsstand in Harvard Square in Cambridge every Tuesday afternoon, waiting for the arrival of the English soccer magazines (*Shoot, Match, World Soccer*) and Monday's *Daily Mirror* and *Telegraph* for in-depth coverage of the weekend's matches. There must be a Red Sox fan in London who goes through a similar routine for *Sporting News* and *USA Today Baseball Weekly*.

Naturally, the tidbits gleaned from such readings are shared with friends at such local soccer watering holes as the Plough and Stars in Cambridge and South Boston's Abbey Tavern. If

Manchester City are featured as "Match of the Day" fodder or if an Old Firm game between Celtic and Rangers is sent from Glasgow, then appropriate sky blue or green-striped scarves are also in order. As my friend Mike LaVigne would say to no one in particular over a pint of freshly drawn Guinness with a game blaring in the background at the Plough and Stars, "Gentlemen, this is soccer heaven."

My teams are Manchester City (perpetual underdogs with a glorious history, not unlike the Red Sox or Chicago Cubs) and Celtic of Glasgow, a team with an even more storied tradition than our local NBA franchise of the same name. I also am a great admirer of Ajax of Amsterdam and Inter-Milan. My favorite national team other than the United States is the plucky squad from the Republic of Ireland, led by that charismatic Geordie Giant Jack Charlton. My left shin still bears a scar from the folding chair that was kicked against my leg at the Plough and Stars in the jubilation of a hundred Irish fans who danced around and shouted at a television screen that showed Packie Bonner save a crucial penalty against Romania in Genoa. It sent the "Boys in Green" to the quarter finals of the 1990 World Cup.

Discovering the Game

> Football is a simple game. The hard part is making it look simple.
>
> Ron Greenwood, England Manager, c. 1978

As a kid growing up in Worcester, Massachusetts, in the sixties, I first discovered the game indirectly through reading about my brother's heroics in his high school yearbook, which chronicled his play as a star fullback for the Westminster School in Simsbury, Connecticut. In our neighborhood soccer was the preserve of private school kids who either were too small for the football team or were cut from the same but were required to play a fall sport. My brother, seven years my senior, was neither too small nor unskilled in the ways of his idol Y.A. Tittle and his beloved New York Football Giants. He played soccer only after injuring his hand in a pre-season football scrimmage to the extent that he would miss most of the season. Desiring both an outlet for his adolescent fires and a sport that would allow him to play with his bandaged hand, he became a dogged defender who scored more than his share of goals. To this day he is still the only player I have ever seen play the game in prescription Wayfarer sunglasses (in all conditions) bound with a Saf-T-Guard. By the age of twelve, the only two soccer players I had ever heard of were Pelé and Robert Flynn Johnson.

In the days before youth soccer became a pubescent right of passage, the only soccer played informally on my street was usually led by a neighbor, son of a local baker who had emigrated from Sweden, or by my brother and his prep school buddies. Prior to each game a much abused Sportcraft soccer ball was taken from its hiding place in my brother's closet, to the right of his baseball cards and above several boxes of teenage booty, the likes of which included a genuine machete, a stack of *Mad* magazines, and a baseball autographed by the 1962 San Francisco Giants. By the time the sacred ball (made in Brazil, no less!) appeared on our front lawn, four piles of jackets and sweatshirts (which sometimes would also include an abandoned football or baseball glove) formed opposing goalposts for frenzied games of three on three. Such contests were heavy on sliding tackles, handballs, extreme challenges and vocal histrionics. Although this action was hardly the equal to that witnessed on the backstreets of Glasgow or the sands of Ipanema the exuberance, joy and camaraderie of those moments all contributed to my love for, and near-obsession with, the game.

Within several years I too was treading the fields of the Independent School League, first as a junior high schooler at Bancroft School and later as a third-team player at Lawrence Academy in Groton, Massachusetts. Never remotely as skilled as my brother, I played the game as an enthusiastic 5'11", 125-pound center half, whose main attribute was an ability to run all day without crashing into teammates. However, I had a tendency to react to most balls in a manner most closely resembling Martin Short doing his best portrayal of Ed Grimley or Don Knotts as Barney Fife removing his gun from its holster. Despite the unintentional on-field levity no one had more fun playing the game or respected the skills required to master the game more than I did. Is there any sport where it is as tough to score and where the execution of a decent non-scoring play such as a pass or header is more gratifying?

Before long, the game I loved as a player won my heart as a fan through the incredible action and emotion associated with one memorable game, namely the 1970 FA Cup Final. That game, which ended in a tie that necessitated a rematch a week later, was a classic that featured Don Revie's marauding Leeds United hoard versus Chelsea, the stylish underdogs from London. It was pure coincidence that found me in front of the tube one Saturday morning in late spring of 1970 as Jim McKay and the "Wide World of Sports" broadcast the first game live from Wembley Stadium. The build-up to the action was tremendous, McKay describing Chelsea as the soccer equivalent of baseball's Miracle Mets from the previous autumn. The soccer culture of England was introduced to me through this most memorable of matches; and if I could select the single sporting event I would most like to attend in the entire world, I would find it impossible to pass up the second Saturday in May at Wembley Stadium.

Aches and Pains

All that I know most surely about morality and the obligations of man, I owe to football.

—Albert Camus, French Philosopher-Novelist, who kept goal for Oran Football Club in Algeria

The ultimate escalation of my re-discovery of soccer in 1989 was the inevitable search in the back of my closet for my twenty-year-old adidas LaPlatas, which I knew would fit, even if the rest of the old uniform didn't. Alas, the shoes had been relegated along with three complete years of *The Hockey News* and an untold number of Topps baseball cards to the local landfill! After springing for a discounted pair of Copas and having selected a suitable Celtic Football Club T-shirt, I began training in earnest at a local high school, several stone beyond my youth and more than several steps behind the pace of my last pitch appearance. Fortunately my practice field contained an antiquated soccer backboard, the better to pretend I was Jinky Johnstone or Charlie Nicholas while making perfect passes to imaginary teammates and silencing the Ibrox multitude with unstoppable shots to the top corner of the Ranger net.

My eventual destination was the venerable Over the Hill League, America's largest and best over-thirty soccer league. After several phone calls I hooked up with the Westwood team and for one spring season didn't embarrass myself too much while having a lot of fun in a Sunday morning ritual that was at once an expression of my true love of the game and an exercise in mortality.

Off the field I also became involved with the creation of some local and national soccer history as I along with such Boston soccer luminaries as Mike LaVigne, Riedar Tryggestad, Rick Copland, Peter Counsell, Tom Bagley, and Chris O'Connell, formed a committee that not only got the ball rolling on the historic USA vs Ireland match at Foxboro Stadium in 1991, but also created the Sports Museum Challenge Cup featuring the U.S. Women's National Team against Norway.

Both games in the two-game Challenge Cup series before a combined record-breaking crowd of more than 12,000 were played with an intensity uncommon to most international "friendlies." Each squad was preparing for the inaugural women's world championships to be played a few months later in China. Each was keen on testing the other in this *de facto* dress rehearsal for the world championships. Even their practices were as intense and purposeful as any game.

I have never felt prouder of any group I have worked with than I did when standing shoulder to shoulder with our organizing committee presenting the first Sports Museum Challenge Cup to Norway at Tufts University in September of 1991. Here was proof positive that a small group of soccer lovers could attempt the impossible and succeed.

Two months later, both Norway and the U.S. emerged finalists from a sixteen-team draw in China after a fortnight of action. Unlike the action at our Challenge Cup, where Norway won decisively, the United States rode on the back of striker extraordinaire Michelle Akers-Stahl, who pounced on an errant backpass with two minutes left in regulation to hand Norway a stunning one-nil defeat.

In a tavern twelve thousand miles removed from Guagzhou Stadium, toasts were offered in honor of both teams by friends who could only wonder at the extremes of joy and sorrow being experienced by our sisters at the summit. As Reidar Tryggestad would comment more than once when contemplating the quicksilver fickleness of the beautiful world game, "The ball is round." Indeed.

Epilogue

In March of 1992 Boston was designated one of nine venues for the 1994 World Cup. Plans were also hatched for the renewal of the second annual Sports Museum Challenge Cup as well as the first annual National Women's Soccer festival to be hosted by our match committee in suburban Boston. Soccer heaven, once experienced secondhand in front of the Trinitron at the Plough, was becoming reality before our eyes! The world game was back.

Their Gift To Me

PAUL E. HARRIS, JR.

I'll never forget the look on those faces. The total happiness. All eight of them. Probably the first soccer ball they ever owned. Just a minute before, they had posed with me after the greatest soccer game ever played. What a game it was on a remote beach in Mexico.

It was a weekend away from home, and why the ball came along is still a mystery. We went there to be alone, to sit in the sun. But I decided to take a run on this open, secluded expanse, first with the ball under my arm, then at my feet; dribbling, feinting, alone in my enduring pleasure.

Where they came from I'll never know. In less than a minute it seemed like a pack, then a regiment, all against one ex-goalkeeper with fading skills. Soon we chose up sides, with a towel or two marking out a goal. No rules, just smiling kids and a soccer nut showing his skills. Sometimes the ball was given up deliberately, but they never knew it.

The game must have lasted a full hour, we were all tired, but no one admitted it. Time to stop, to move on, with skills exhausted. But first a picture, then the great announcement: "La pelota es para ustedes. Es para todos." ("The ball is for you, for all of you.")

That game was my greatest soccer experience. Not because of

35

the warm sun, the quiet beach, and the happy chatter above the waves. Here, I had found the real game, and those *amigos* allowed me the full retreat to my own youth. There was no way I could keep the ball. It was a gift in return for the gift that had come my way. Leaving the beach, I turned for one last moment, and watched them sharing the ball.

Without a Country or
a Name in Haiti

Frank Dell'Apa

One hot August night, we were planning a walk to the Hotel Oloffson for a nightcap. That was when The Man Without A Country informed us that if we tried to do so, we would be lying dead in the street within minutes of our proposed departure.

He offered to drive us, and we arrived in time to order bottles of Prestige beer, just before the electricity failed and Port-au-Prince went completely dark. We sped back to our hotel, chased by wild dogs. The Man Without A Country cursed as the car swerved.

During the day, the city had been very much alive. Youngsters wearing the red stockings of the national team pulled high-kicked balls in the park off the Rue de Champ de Mars. The streets—named for John Brown, Jean-Jacques Dessalines, Jean-Paul II, Martin Luther King, Haile Selassie—teemed with people. The colorful tap-tap trucks, which provide much of the public transportation, raced about filled with people.

That evening we fell into conversation with The Man Without A Country at the hotel bar. He was Lebanese-Haitian. He could not, he said, return to Lebanon. Nor, apparently, was Haiti safe, since within weeks it would explode in a military coup.

At some point, the subject switched from corrupt govern-

38

ments and the plight of oppressed people. The United States, someone said, would be playing host to the World Cup in 1994. "That being the case," said The Man Without a Country, "I predict that the U.S. will win the World Cup by 1998, or 2002 at the latest. Now that Americans are playing football, they will be the best."

The bartender, who seemed to have been asleep on his feet when we arrived, had not previously responded to any of our conversation, though he had spoken some Creole in hushed tones to The Man Without A Country. Suddenly, he declared: "The Americans will win the World Cup in 1994."

The next night, Stade Silvio Cator was jammed with 40,000 people. The stadium's namesake had been possibly the world's most remarkable athlete of his era. Silvio Cator was the first man to exceed 26 feet in the long jump, in 1930; he was also captain of Haiti's national team in soccer. There have been many larger-than-life figures in Haitian history and many of them are re-membered by statues in the Place des Héros de l'Indépendance. But the largest monument to a national hero is the stadium it-self.

Thousands had entered the stadium early in the afternoon, exposing themselves to the baking summer sun. We entered through the locker room and were greeted by the insistent sounds of Boukman Eksperyans blasting from portable speakers. By the 6 p.m. kickoff, the stadium was overflowing, and fans were literally holding onto the floodlight stanchions above the walls for a view of the match.

The atmosphere was charged as ever in Port-au-Prince. "Sim-mering," said The Man Without A Country.

Jean-Claude Nord, the gigantic president of the Fédération Haitienne de Football, greeted us with a flourish of Creole and then sat in a large green-vinyl chair. We went to field level to copy the lineups from a radio announcer, who could have been in his teens. Dozens of curious Haitians crowded around us.

There were hints that Jean-Bertrand Aristide would attend the match. The American Embassy people feared that he "would cause too much commotion" and were relieved that he never appeared.

Just after the match started, we noticed the radio announcer talking excitedly and rapidly behind us, still surrounded by dozens of young men.

The young American players were clearly shocked by the speedy aggressiveness of the Haitians but held firm and counterattacked. The Haitians deflated following a missed opportunity. The Americans took the lead as Dante Washington scored from a long through ball. Lightning bolts filled the sky and the predictable soaking rainstorm crashed over the Montagne Noire.

Glass bottles shattered off the goal and littered the net behind the American goalkeeper. The Trinidadian linesman took a stone to the back of the head. Jean-Claude Nord bustled from his comfortable chair down to the playing field and personally appointed a substitute linesman. The stadium cleared out during the delay. The Americans scored again, then streamed into the locker room.

The Racing Club bus, brightly painted like the tap-taps, pulled up to the locker room door. Security men from the U.S. Embassy quickly funneled in coaches and players. As we approached the gates, stones crashed against the windows and the driver's head was split open. The bus careened through the crowds, past the statue of the Marron Inconnu, and delivered us to the hotel.

A mere Olympic qualifying match had become quite eventful. The next day, The Man Without A Country took us back to the Oloffson to meet Aubelin Jolicoeur.

Jolicoeur, Petit Pierre in Graham Greene's novel, *The Comedians*, has been a court jester and journalist, and who knows what else. He told us of seeing Joe Gaetjens play against an all-star team in 1943 at Parc Le Conte, which would later be renamed to honor Silvio Cator.

"Joe was like a god to me," Jolicoeur said. "I didn't hear about him again until he scored the goal in the World Cup. We were so happy!"

Jolicoeur attempted to explain what had happened to Gaetjens and other Haitians since those happier times. But there seemed to be no satisfactory explanation. Haiti had become a land filled with fear and suspicion, its great spirit tested by awesome influences from the outside and cruel forces within.

When we began the search for Joe Gaetjens, we had little to go on except pictures of him facing Bert Williams with the ball in the back of the English net; Gaetjens smiling as he is borne on the shoulders of the Brazilian fans, plus the accounts of those who were in Mineiro Stadium in Belo Horizonte, Brazil, when the U.S. defeated England, 1–0, June 29, 1950, in the most unimaginable of upsets. Most reports of the game were filled with incredulity. The British thought the goal was a complete accident. Gaetjens' teammates attributed the score to Gaetjens' resourcefulness. In any case, the goal had assured Gaetjens' name of a semblance of immortality.

Gaetjens' story after that game is less clear. He played professionally in Paris and Montpellier, with and against legends such as Ernst Happel; one year, he offered to return his salary because he had not performed to his own expectations. He returned to Haiti, opened a chain of dry cleaning stores and became a celebrity spokesman for Colgate-Palmolive. In July 1963 he was arrested in front of his store on Rue Pavée, taken to Fort Dimanche prison and, presumably, executed.

However, no death certificate exists for Gaetjens. There has been no official acknowledgment of his arrest or imprisonment, or even his existence, by the government. Maybe he remained alive, living in anonymity somewhere in the Haitian countryside?

"It is impossible to think that Joe Gaetjens is still alive," said The Man Without A Country. "Haiti is a small place. Everyone knows everyone else."

We were guided by The Man Without A Country to the Rue Pavée, where the dry cleaners had been located. The blue-painted two-story building was boarded up, as were most buildings on the block. We left the city, driving past what is referred to as the La Saline slum, an open-sewered mud flat inhabited by thousands of people living in flimsy huts. The painted sign before a one-room wooden shack declared: "Big Bank Samuele Borlette." Another sign announced: "City Martyrs di Fort Dimanche."

Within minutes, we turned onto a dirt road. The area was deserted except for an underfed bull, which straggled through the weedy swamp. The prison was empty, its terror chambers having been closed after the Duvaliers departed, and sounds echoed.

The barren cells in the dull, orange-painted cinder block buildings were numbered. The men's quarters were about 15 feet square with cement floors. The only visible difference in the women's quarters was small openings at the top of the walls, apparently for ventilation purposes. Names and phrases had been written in pencil on the walls. In cell No. 9 were the words: "Espoir Fait Vivre."

"At midnight," The Man Without A Country said, "they would call a name. That person would write his name on the wall and they would take him behind another wall."

He led us toward a courtyard.

"They would stand them against this wall," he said. "And shoot them."

This, then, was where Joe Gaetjens had been killed. Far from the magical Mineiro Stadium, where the joyous Brazilians had carried him off the field. Far from the modern boulevards of Paris, far from New York City, where he established a reputation as a bon vivant.

Gaetjens' family has sought justice. He had apparently never faced criminal charges, leaving no justification for his arrest, much less his death. But, since no records were available, Gaetjens could only be treated as a missing person for seven years following the reporting of his absence. Or so Gaetjens wife, Lyliane, was told.

Gaetjens' brother, Gérard, who would be assassinated by *zenglendos*, or bandits, the week before we arrived in 1991, had pulled political strings. The family established a Joe Gaetjens Foundation in New Hampshire. The Organization of American

States and the Human Rights Commission made inquiries. A benefit match was organized by Clive Toye and the New York Cosmos in 1972. When Gaetjens' son, Richard, grew old enough to learn the truth, he returned to Port-au-Prince, searched out his father's executioners, and confronted them. He wrote a play about his father's final days, and there was hope that Sean Connery would have a role.

"His two best friends killed him," said Richard Gaetjens, who has an acting career in Los Angeles. "I talked to the one who pulled the trigger. He did not tell me that he shot him. He just put his hands up in the air.

"What happened in Haiti is, with the change of governments, there was a change in the attitudes of the people. People became involved in the military, which gives power to those who had never had power at all."

Joe Gaetjens was an inspiring sporting figure, of divine stature to his countrymen. In the end, though, he was like thousands and millions of other Haitians who have met inexplicable and unaccountable death. They are People Without Names. Their spirit lives on.

Soccer Intersections:
A Story of Lives, Teams, and Hearts

Doug Chapman

In England it's likely that one could guess which football team people support based on where they were brought up.

If you're from Woolwich or Greenwich, in suburban London, your team is mostly likely to be Charlton Athletic. If you're from Islington, it's a safe bet that it's Arsenal.

But what if you're from New England as in Northeastern region of the U.S.—like me?

I must admit that I'm first an Arsenal supporter because of family history and a past Gunners manager named Herbert Chapman. Having the bronze bust of an ancestor in Arsenal's marble hallway makes a difference. But I came to support Charlton purely of my own volition.

First, it was Flanagan. And later, it was the story of The Valley.

The Charlton Valiants, as they are called, had a strong following here over a decade ago. The reasons were simple: Mike Flanagan, Paddy Powell, and Lawrie Abrahams. The trio played for the now sadly defunct New England Tea Men of the NASL. And there were others, some whose names are familiar, some not. But they all played for the Tea Men during the team's three short years of existence in Foxboro and Boston.

None of them had the impact of Mike Flanagan. With his long, curly blond hair, his outgoing manner and his ability to score goals, Mike Flanagan was a star. If soccer in New England had a matinée idol, it was Flanagan. He was the one player most accountable for a burst of soccer popularity in New England in 1978–79. He was also indirectly responsible for the sport's eventual failure to hold a grasp of the public interest in the area.

Flanagan in his one season with the Tea Men scored thirty goals and made eight assists in twenty-eight games. England stood up and took notice of their man making good in the U.S. He was named the NASL's Most Valuable Player in a poll of league players. He received 79 votes, followed by Trevor Francis of the Detroit Express with 48, and Franz Beckenbauer of the New York Cosmos with 33 votes. Flanagan received a new car and a trophy. He was also named the Offensive Player of the Year by the league, for having been named Offensive Star of the Game more than any other NASL player.

"I'm really over the moon about the MVP award," he said at the time. "When I came to play this summer, I couldn't foresee anything like this happening."

The Tea Men played before crowds as high as 30,126 home and 62,497 away. Both of those highwater marks came against the Cosmos, with Flanagan the big match player in each with game-winning goals.

"Everything's so different in football over here," said Keith Weller from Leicester, England, also on the Tea Men. "They actually let the press in the locker rooms, even women reporters. Then there are the stadiums, the scoreboards, the cheerleaders, the bands, the flashing lights, a guy playing the organ. It's different, all right."

England stood up and took notice of their man making good in the U.S. Still having him under contract, Charlton sold him to their South London rival, Crystal Palace. It was very different the following season for the Tea Men without Flanagan. The average Tea Men crowd dwindled to 6,562. The fans' hero was gone, to what sounded to them like a shop specializing in glass antiques. I lost track of Flanagan until the fall of 1988.

Flanagan returned to a rivalry between two teams that would in a few years find itself in turmoil, for in 1985 both Charlton and Crystal Palace began to play their games in the same stadium, Selhurst Park. The Valley, where Charlton had always played, had been condemned. Following the tragic fire that killed 57 people in the wooden grandstand at Bradford City, the Greater London Council began closely inspecting football grounds for safety hazards. The GLC decided to issue a summons against Charlton Athletic for violating the Safety of Sports Gound Act. The Valley's huge East Terrace was closed because it was deemed unsafe. To further complicate matters the owner of the Valley, and formerly Charlton's chairman of the board, Michael Gliksten, decided to fence off the stadium's parking area for what was called "further development." That move denied access to the main stand opposite the now closed East Terrace. Charlton had to find a new stadium, and the search stopped at Selhurst Park, home of arch rival Crystal Palace. Charlton supporters were gutted.

"Football without . . . an identification with bricks and mortar (or even corrugated iron and rotten wood) is like having theatre in a car park," Norman Fox of the *Independent* was later to write. It was the equivalent of being kicked out of the supporters' own homes, because to them, the Valley was home, and they were determined to get it back.

Logistically the move was a nightmare. Emotionally, it was worse. The distance between the Valley and Selhurst Park is only seven miles as the crow flies. However, that distance disguises one of the most difficult urban drives through congested city streets in all of London. There's no direct rail service, and the bus ride takes more than an hour.

Rick Everitt, a Charlton supporter, spearheaded the effort to get the Valley back. The back page of the October 2, 1986 issue of the local paper the *Mercury* had the banner headline, "Our Home Is the Valley," along with a petition for the team's return with more than 15,000 signatures presented to the Charlton directors. Everitt's fanzine *The Voice of the Valley* appeared in February 1988. It began with an editorial describing the derelict state of the Valley:

> There are weeds 3 feet high where Derek Hales claimed goal-scoring records. The goalmouths are choked with greenery more suffocating than any offside trap. The terrace sweeps unevenly along one side, towering still above contrasting stands, but Sam Bartram's gate is padlocked. Nails driven into the doors of rusting turnstiles might as well be driven into supporters' hearts.

The effort to move back received a huge boost in June, 1988 when the club's ownership changed hands. The new co-owners, Roger Alwen and Michael Norris, later purchased The Valley.

That should have been the happy ending, but it wasn't. A fight took extreme twists and turns over the next four-plus seasons as the supporters in seemingly one voice told the directors a return to the Valley was their only priority. Politics entered the picture; there were constant battles with the local council over planning permission; a completely new party—the Valley Party—was founded to campaign in the council election; it had one single issue: getting Charlton back to its rightful home; there was a local strike that delayed things even more; and money had to be raised.

In October of 1988 I went to London to write about the first American College Football Game to be played in Great Britain between my alma mater, Boston University, and the University of Richmond. I also planned on writing at least one article on English soccer.

I decided to go to the Queens Park Rangers game. I told the woman at QPR who I was, what newspaper I represented, what I was doing in England and what I planned to write about. I was told in no uncertain terms that I was not welcome. It seems they expected a contingent of journalists who would also be covering the upcoming International and didn't have room for "an American football writer."

I offered to purchase a ticket if I could have access to interview people after the game. Again, I was denied.

"We don't want or need any American journalists here," she said. "Why don't you try Charlton Athletic. They'd be happy to have anyone at their games."

Charlton Athletic! Sure, why not. An even better choice, I thought. I'd love to see the team that sent us Flanagan. I never had any feeling one way or the other for QPR. I do now, even though the not-very-pleasant women did me a favor in the long run.

I telephoned the Charlton office and was connected with Peter Burrowes. He said I was welcome at Charlton, and he would make the necessary press arrangements. He also told me how I could get to Selhurst Park from my hotel.

Selhurst Park? What happened to the Valley? I didn't know about the condemned stadium. Why would they be playing at rival Crystal Palace's grounds?

During the game I noticed that Charlton's first-team coach was Mike Flanagan. It had to be the same person, which Burrowes confirmed, and he arranged for me to speak with Flanagan after the game. I don't know who was happier, me to meet Flanagan, or Flanagan to see a newspaper man from the area of the States where he was once so popular. Flanagan grabbed a box full of unopened beer cans, and I got a better story than anything that could have happened at QPR.

After playing for Crystal Palace, Flanagan was sold back to Charlton in 1984, and in 1987 a knee injury ended his playing career. He became a scout for Charleton and then a first team coach, which is what he was doing when I saw him at Selhurst Park. But it was not long afterwards that Charlton and Flanagan parted ways. He went off to Southend United and later Gillingham, while Charleton Athletic continued playing in Selhurst and the fight for a return to the Valley wore on.

On December 5, 1992, Charlton fans finally were able to witness a true home match—$3,000,000 later, raised by their own efforts, and after 2,632 days, or seven years and 11 weeks that were lost in a wilderness of ground sharing and away fixtures.

Invited with other former players, Mike Flanagan was there, bringing the memory of the Tea Men along with him in the circuitous journey he had made from the Valley via Boston via Selhurst for one team, then Selhurst for another, and via the other sequences that make up the plays of people's lives.

I was there shortly afterwards. Mark Purcell, a Charlton supporter, best summed up the scene: "For me, it started about an hour into the match. The throat dried up and the tears began to well. It only lasted a few minutes and then it passed and I could enjoy it all again. But for those few short moments, it had suddenly got to me . . . we were home."

THE VALLEY

(sung on the terraces to the
tune of "Mull of Kintyre")

Many miles have I travelled
Many games have I seen
Following Charlton
My favourite team.
Many hours have I spent
In the Covered End choir
Singing, Valley, Floyd Road,
My only desire,
Valley, Floyd Road,
The mist rolling in from the Thames.
My only desire is always to be there
At Valley, Floyd Road.

Don't Hack the Ball

ANN ADAMS

In the spring of 1969, my family moved from Whitehouse, Ohio, to South Ascot, England, where we were to spend the next 2½ years. During that time, my twin and I attended Swinley Primary, a public school with students primarily of working class origins. While I learned a variety of subjects at Swinley, I will always remember it most fondly as the place where I learned to play soccer. In fact, if it hadn't been for soccer, we would have remained "foreigners" for a long time. Even more than the accents we adopted, soccer became an avenue for assimilation and acceptance.

Of course, soccer, or football as we called it then, is as big in England as baseball or football is in America. Kids grow up kicking the ball around much sooner than they learn to throw it. I was seven when we moved, and my experience playing baseball far outweighed my soccer expertise. Soccer had not really made its way to the Midwest in the late sixties, so my soccer experiences were limited to the occasional game in gym class.

The first day of school was an anxious time, of course. I'd moved before and I knew what it was like to be the new kid on the block. I hated it. Being in a different culture made it worse. I had thought that it wouldn't be that much different, since the English spoke English, but I was wrong. Our second grade

49

teacher assigned some poor girl named Monica to make our first day less trying. Monica's task was to keep us happy, and she was warned of severe repercussions if we weren't smiling at the end of the day. So motivated, she showed us around the schoolyard during recess.

One of the first things that my twin, Eve, and I noticed in the schoolyard was that a very competitive soccer game seemed to be the main event of recess, at least for the boys. The girls seemed content to stand in small groups and talk, or play quietly in their neat, gray jumpers. We watched from the sidelines until the ball was booted out of bounds and rolled to our feet. A boy ran over and yelled at us in a broad Cockney accent, "Pass it 'ere, then." Eve attempted to comply, but accidentally sent the ball in another direction. The boy, thoroughly disgusted by what he perceived to be a deliberate attempt to make him run more than he had to, said, "Shut up," then ran after the ball. Eve looked startled and mentioned to Monica that she hadn't said anything to the boy. Monica informed Eve that "shut up" was synonymous with "stop it" in our new neighborhood. This information only served to heighten our sense of alienation and isolation.

As the weeks passed, we grew used to our new school uniforms and became more adept at understanding the Cockney dialect that most of the school spoke. We also gained some friends, to whom we began to teach the rudiments of baseball. They reciprocated by teaching us how to play soccer, rugby, and cricket. While we played sandlot variations of all those games, only soccer was played competitively at the elementary level. When my brothers graduated to grammar school (high school), they began to play rugby and cricket in school, but Eve and I dedicated ourselves to soccer. Eventually we became quite proficient at dribbling, passing, stealing, and shooting the ball. Our teachers, the boys in our class, demanded a sophistication that required effort and practice on our part. We were constantly reprimanded for our crude kicking style, "hacking at the ball," because kicking someone else in the shin (whether accidentally or not) when trying to steal the ball from them was considered loutish and unacceptable.

As Eve and I gained male friends, Monica was relieved of her chaperoning duties. In fact, because we were tomboys, the other girls shunned Eve and me. There was a clear separation of boys and girls within the school system, and we had inadvertently stepped over social boundaries. None of the girls would talk to us, because we played soccer with the boys. They were further appalled to see us disrobing at recess. Eve and I had decided that the gray pinafore jumpers and button shirts that we had to wear as part of the school uniform were entirely too restrictive. To rectify this situation, we decided to wear our soccer shorts underneath our jumpers and at recess strip down to just the shorts. Since the boys also took their shirts off to play, they accepted our action with equanimity, but the girls never forgave us for such uncouth behavior.

The soccer field proved to be a good place to learn. It was on the field that I first learned how to say "fuck" and what it meant. In fact, I would venture to say that "fuck," in all of its adverbial, adjectival, and verbal constructs, was used on the average every thirty seconds. While we had certainly been privy to the more traditional "shit," "goddam," and "hell" of the American schoolyard, "fuck" was definitely a new acquisition, and we embraced it gleefully. Because we were willing to play hard and swear profusely, the boys accepted us.

Of course, there was still the need to maintain some semblance of "normal" male/female relations. Thus, when we weren't playing soccer, Eve and I would go into the bushes with one of our "boyfriends" and kiss. Ironically, though, those sessions were just as unusual as our disrobing on the fields, because usually the boys and girls didn't do such things. These types of encounters usually occurred in grammar school when adolescent hormones kicked in and the two sexes began to converge. Maybe our boyfriends' older brothers had told them what to do with girls who spent time with them. But, it hadn't taken. Because of our age, we would all quickly become bored with the kissing activity and get back to the fun stuff. Soccer.

The only other female who played soccer was Phillipa; she was a thalidomide baby. These are the children whose mothers took thalidomide, a sedative causing severe malformations in their children. Phillipa was born without arms, but she did have a finger-like appendage growing out of each shoulder joint which she used to suck on, just as I would suck my thumb. One would think that soccer would be the perfect sport for someone missing her arms, as no one but the goalie is allowed to touch the ball with their hands. Of course, goalie is the position that Phillipa insisted on playing.

I vividly remember how she would dive to head the ball out of the way when someone would take a shot at the goal. She would go sliding over the ground using every part of her body to block the ball. Once she had possession, she would lie on top of the ball until everyone backed off, so she could kick it. She also had a penchant for playing in her barefeet, because she found that shoes cut off her sensitivity. Although I'm sure Phillipa had very tough feet, I would always wince at the sight and sound of bare toes on hard leather when she'd clear the ball from the goal area.

Phillipa would come from the field to the dining room for our lunch. The cooking staff would set up tables and chairs in the assembly room, each table accommodating six children. We would sit at the table and wait for the staff to serve the main course on china and the headmistress to offer a prayer. Phillipa would prop her filthy soccer feet on the table in front of her and begin to eat by holding her utensils between her big and second toes. Her flexibility and coordination were astonishing.

Soccer gave to me, Eve, and Phillipa what our status as Americans and differently-abled could not. It provided a community, a niche in a culture that would otherwise have shunned us for being other. For that reason, I believe that the greatest offering competitive sports has is community.

But not everyone felt as enthusiastic about soccer as we did, and my mother did not always support our decision to play. For three hours each Friday afternoon at Swinley, the girls and boys would be divided so that the boys would go out to the soccer field to play soccer, while the girls stayed in the classroom to sew. To her credit, the headmistress recognized that Eve and I were unique cases, more as Americans than as tomboys, and so she approached my mother with the question of whether she should include us with the girls or the boys. Such a breach in the usual rigidity of the English school system was atypical. Unfortunately, Eve and I didn't know the headmistress had asked. My mother made the executive decision that we should learn how to sew, because we already knew how to play soccer well enough. She told the headmistress to keep us in the sewing class and only mentioned her part in the plot years later. I'm sure there were times when the headmistress wondered if my mother had made the right decision, because Eve and I never completed a single assignment except for the one in which we could choose any sewing task. While the other girls worked at ornate embroidery, Eve and I slowly and painfully cut two strips of white cloth and attached them to our blue soccer shorts. For this effort we were awarded an overall grade of D- instead of a well-deserved F.

Despite our loss of practice time, Eve and I continued to improve from our daily recess play and the weekend pick-up games. When we did return to America in 1971 at the age of ten, we probably had better ball-handling skills than most American kids three to four years older than we. With our English accents and obsession with soccer, we arrived at Haskins Elementary in Ohio, where we were perceived as English despite our claims to American citizenship. We continued to wear our school uniforms, much to the pity of our peers, who thought we were so poor we couldn't afford a more varied wardrobe. We also continued to wear our shorts under the uniforms so we could disrobe at recess.

Again, because of our status as other, different, the school administration turned a blind eye to what they might otherwise have condemned as inappropriate behavior. And because of our prowess on the soccer field, we quickly made friends with the boys, and just as quickly were ostracized by the girls. Soccer became our means of readjusting to America, just as it had been our introduction to a new culture. Within six months we had lost our English accents and begun to vary our clothing, although we remained staunch in our right to take our shirts off at recess, just as the boys did. And with time the level of play also dramatically improved. Eve and I demonstrated finesse to our American peers and demanded more from them, just as our English mentors had required it of us. In fact, at my high school graduation, one of my male peers said to me, "I still remember you and your sister when you showed up from England. You'd talk so fast we couldn't understand you with your accents. The only thing we were sure you were saying was, 'Don't 'ack the ball, then.'"

While I have always been grateful for the role all sports have played in my life, offering me a route to increased skill and self-esteem and a sense of belonging, soccer will always be special to me because it represents a time in my childhood when I was beginning to explore the world around me. Indeed, soccer remains the foremost image of that period in my life, and it stays with me even as I continue to play the game today. It was the first activity to which I wanted to commit myself. I had played various games with my brothers for hours on end before moving to England, but I played those games because everyone else did. In England, soccer was my way to release the boundless energy of my seven-year-old displaced self. So my memories of England are not the numerous historical locations we visited, but the playing field at Swinley, surrounded by gorse bushes, and the feel of the wind on my face as I tore down the field, striving to score the goal that would make me the hero of recess.

PART II

SOCCER LINES

Unseen, American Soccer, Unsung

Philip J. Scrofani

How wondrous is he, to levitate a ball on shin and foot and knee,
and thus to carry it so swiftly down corridors of green,
parallel to sidelines, where spectator is seldom seen.
To glide through defenders, like a skater borne on steely blades,
swaying fullbacks from their balance like bending reeds, a soft wind
    over everglades.
Where on plains in Italy, a stadium would roar to the timing of his
    skill,
on the lonely green of Virginia, absent spectators, all is still.
And as fading sun blackens daylight's very soul, his perfect cross
    caroms off his teammate's head.
And a solitary voice yells—goal!

Inside Chapel

PAUL BISHOP

[The following passages are excerpts from *Chapel of the Ravens*, Paul Bishop's novel of international intrigue and mystery that surround the murder of a well-known Italian soccer goalie in Los Angeles. Setting the stage for his eventual move to Los Angeles, the great English goal-keeper, Ian Chapel, remembers the fateful World Cup qualifying game between England and Germany. It was raining hard, and Chapel had to deal with his nemesis Kurt Wagstaff of Germany, who took two shots on goal.]

There is a soccer tradition that goalkeepers and left wingers are insane. It is a popular myth with some basis in fact. But while I might have one or two screws loose, Wagstaff had a complete Erector Set shaking free in his head. In my book, he was positively certifiable. His determination to score often over-rode all physical impossibilities, and although modern playing tactics have made the left wing position almost extinct, Wagstaff has kept the breed alive with his hard-driving finesse and style. He was easily the most dangerous scoring threat on the West German team, and was possessed by a frightening, demented frustration when he failed to put the ball in the back of the net.

*　*　*

The play had drawn me all the way over to the right goalpost, so I received a nasty shock when Lampy [England's center half] slipped in the mud and Kruger [Germany's center forward] deftly lobbed the ball in a high arc across the goal mouth. I scrambled backwards and came out of the net to try and punch the ball away. But even as I jumped, I knew I wasn't going to be in time. Without looking, I knew Wagstaff would be behind me, his head rising like a ground-to-air missile aimed at the ball. A split second later there was the solid thud of forehead meeting ball leather and Wagstaff sent a head shot streaking for the lower left corner of the net.

Inexplicably, I knew the ball could be stopped. Physically I was exhausted, but my mind refused to accept defeat. Reactions, honed by years of practice, took control of my body and snapped it backwards across the face of the goal like a rubber band. My arms and legs were fully extended, fingers straining for the touch of rounded leather, and in that moment I knew the true joy of my chosen profession. It was an exhilaration beyond the highest level of consciousness. I was perfectly performing something for which I had been destined since the spark of my conception. I watched the ball as it bounced once in front of the goal line, and then my fists reached it and punched it around the outside of the goalpost for the save.

*　*　*

. . . Everything seemed to be moving at half speed as I watched Wagstaff jump toward the ball. He was sure of his victory, as if it were a move he had practiced over and over until it was second nature.

From somewhere beyond reason, I was again flooded with the knowledge that I could stop the ball. I dove blindly toward it even as Wagstaff's foot slashed forward with terrifying power. The tips of my gnarled fingers touched the rough surface of the ball, but my arms refused to respond and gather it into me.

Sliding through the mud on a collision course, I could only watch in horror as Wagstaff's shooting foot changed targets with an infinitesimal movement and collided with my face.

*　*　*

[*Sir Adam Qwale, British Army Intelligence, is talking with the once-great English keeper, Ian Chapel, who now blinded in one eye from Wagstaff's kick, has retired from soccer. Sir Adam's aim is to persuade the former goalie to return to the game, albeit indoors and in Los Angeles, to take the place of the murdered Ravens keeper. He fails to mention that Wagstaff also plays for the Ravens.*]

"I wouldn't care if you were fully blind. Or if you had no arms or legs. This is football we're talking about, soccer if you like. Countries have stopped wars for the game. It is bigger than any one person. Bigger than any one team. I love the game. You love the game. No matter what you say, it's in your blood. You suckled it in with your mother's milk. If something threatens the game, we have to do whatever we can to save it."

He paused and I just stared at him.

* * *

[*Ian Chapel plays his first game with the Ravens. He makes a comparison between indoor and outdoor games.*]

. . . The indoor game was not merely a substitute for its more popular outdoor relative, nor was it some second-rate sport for broken-down footballers. I learned rapidly that indoor soccer demands that every skill learned in outdoor soccer be speeded up and honed to perfection. There was no margin for error.

The game also demanded additional skills as players rebounded passes and shots off the boards with consummate perfection. Set plays were used far more often than in outdoor soccer, and defensive players were expected to constantly push forward on offense as well.

Goalkeepers, in particular, had a far more demanding position to play. Within three minutes, I'd already been called on to stop five shots. In some outdoor games, I wouldn't have been called on to stop five shots during the whole ninety minutes. The pace of the game was tremendous, like being inside a giant soccer pinball machine being played by an expert.

Soccer Lovers

Diane M. Russwurm

There's a lot happening on the sidelines of a soccer game, starting with the cries: of ecstasy, happiness, of anguish and anger. The sounds of soccer lovers. And it's all going on before the eyes of a Higher Authority that absolutely detests soccer. Games are not played on perfect, sunny 70-degree days with just a hint of a breeze and a low humidity level. Instead, soccer lovers agonize through meteorological nightmares that push both body and soul to the limits of human endurance. From such cataclysmic conditions as subzero wind chill factors, fiery heat, and underwear-dampening drizzle, comes the belief that soccer lovers are always being subjected to a test of their faith. Perhaps if everyone solemnly vowed to perform charitable deeds, that perfect 70-degree day would for once be granted to soccer lovers before they go to heaven.

Which brings us to the game played in hell. Geographically, soccer hell is located a *minimum* of an hour's drive away on a poorly kept field somewhere behind an abandoned loading dock. This facility is not equipped with even a single portajohn. The opposing team appears to have the genetic makeup of some superhuman species, and they live up to their name of the Mutilators or Hannibal's Cannibals or the Demon Seeds. Just about everyone in the crowd on your side risks being carded, as the opinion that the ref's eyes are closed is expressed—aloud and much more graphically. When the rain comes and the game assumes the flavor of mud wrestling night at the Go-Go-Rama, the inevitable happens: one of your players scores a goal for the other side. The final whistle blows, and there is no more than a collective sigh on the sidelines, one of relief this time, as the soccer lovers pack up and go home, filled with forgiveness and the promise of another day at a field far away.

Play American Soccer

STUART MURRAY

It was a glorious summer evening, and the soccer field was a green carpet on a hill overlooking the central New York town of Oneonta. It was a perfect setting for soccer, but the two semi-professional teams were playing only a slow, pretend game.

It was an exhibition match. The players passed the ball safely back and forth, neither team attacking the goal. Nobody was risking injury in a game that did not count.

The crowd in the stands above that pretty field was thoroughly American, mostly young, suburban, and very polite. They sat munching Crackerjacks and drinking soda, staring curiously, as if something were happening down on the field. They seemed not to mind that the game was, well, as the soccer-bashers say, "dull."

Of course, to real fans, no soccer game is dull. It's always interesting to watch anyone try to play. In the case of these two teams, there was plenty of ability, but none of the players seemed interested in giving the fans a show. As long as no one objected, the teams just went through the motions. Players passed the ball back and forth across the field. Down to the stopper. Look. Across to the fullback. Push it to the goalie. Pick it up. Look. Roll it to the other fullback, who sends it across to the opposite midfielder. Kill the ball. Look. Start the slow dance once again.

The teams took turns leading this dance, while the fans sat with their Crackerjacks and soda, chewing and staring. As far as the fans were concerned, it might as well have been television they were watching, for they had nothing to say to the players unless there was a shot on goal, which happened every fifteen minutes or so, and then they just said, "Oooh." If this had been any town outside America the teams would have been roundly booed for their charade. But American soccer fans are polite.

Then, high up in the center of the stands a middle-aged man began to yell at the players. Since he was the only one in the whole stadium raising his voice, everyone heard him.

"Come on, you guys, show us what you've got! Come on, make it exciting. Play hard! You're putting us to sleep!"

Naturally, this yeller disturbed many Oneonta fans, and some turned around to give him looks of annoyance. He knew they thought him no better than some drunken hockey fan, but he had a point to make. A soccer point.

He was not normally rowdy. He was much like the rest of the Oneonta fans—middle-class and suburban, a good father. He was also a high school soccer coach who never abused referees. But he believed the people in the stadium ought to know that they were seeing sham soccer, and he felt they ought to object loudly.

The players and coaches, mostly foreign-born, obviously thought no one in the stands knew any better. But the yeller knew better, and he was telling them so.

"Come on, guys, play soccer!" he roared. "Give these people a show! You can do it! Show them good soccer!"

Granted, the game was just an exhibition, but it was meant to be the centerpiece of a celebration sponsored by the National Soccer Hall of Fame, which stands in downtown Oneonta. In the crowd were a number of elderly men who had been inducted into the Hall of Fame that weekend. The festivities were in honor of their contribution to American soccer over the past seventy years. This game was disrespectful to these tough, old fellows, most of whom looked as if they could still step on the field and drill one home.

The Soccer Hall of Fame is in the heart of very good soccer country, where collegiate powerhouses Hartwick and Oneonta play each fall to the enthusiastic cheers of their fans. This was, in fact, the Hartwick field being used for the game. But there was no cheering this evening, only the steady teasing of the fan with his private soccer point to make.

It didn't do much good. The teams did not play any harder, despite his yelling. No fans joined in to urge the teams on, and none of the hall-of-famers offered to go out and show them how to do it right. It was a disappointment for the yeller.

Then, he had an inspiration: "Play American Soccer!" he bellowed. "Play American soccer, if you know what that is!"

He had been born in Scotland but brought up in New Jersey, playing hard and fast soccer—high school, college, and then semi-pro. American soccer. He knew how exciting the American game could be, and that's why he bellowed again, "Play American soccer, will you!"

Some high school kids nearby grinned and glanced at each other. They didn't get it. After all, wasn't American soccer the lousiest in the world?

"Play American soccer!" he yelled again, feeling sure he was beginning to get his message across to the players. And sure enough, they were picking up their game. Did they sense his challenge? What about the few American players on the field? At least two were on the U.S. national team. Would they at least rise to the occasion?

"Play American soccer!"

The pace of the players quickened, the ball coming to life. Now the yeller felt better, and he sat back to enjoy the game after one last "Play American soccer!" rang across the field, this time almost triumphantly.

Then, a woman's voice floated over the crowd, speaking ever

so slowly, so that the words hung in the air when she said,
"What's that? Kickball?"

Her voice was quite soft, yet clear enough for hundreds of
spectators to hear.

What's that? Kickball?

Oh, how it stung!

What's that? Kickball?

Kickball! The game in which a ball is rolled to the "batter,"
who kicks it wildly and runs around the bases. No, what the
woman really meant was "kick-and-run"—soccer without skill.
American soccer!

Yet she meant to insult the yeller, not American soccer.

She and most of the crowd actually thought this *was* skillful
soccer they were watching. After all, these players were mostly
foreigners, and foreigners are all good soccer players, right? Better than Americans, anyway, right?

No doubt the lady with the soft, carrying voice loved soccer,
or she wouldn't have been at the game. She probably had a couple of kids in the local league and was a loyal supporter of school
and club teams. She probably sliced oranges for halftime, and
her husband probably helped line the field. She probably always
did more than her share of trucking kids back and forth to
games and practices, week after week, month after month.

She probably loved soccer and the idea of having the young
Soccer Hall of Fame in her hometown. She was probably a true
soccer mother, one of a new generation of fans, salt of the soccer
earth and pillar of the soccer house of worship.

And now there was a lout in the stands during an exhibition
game that was commemorating her very own Hall of Fame.

American soccer? You mean kickball?

Arrgh! How little she knew about American soccer. How little
respect for the tough, smart and exciting play, the courage and
heroics of past American players, some of whom were sitting
gray-headed, just a few rows away. Wasn't this whole exhibition,
this whole weekend, honoring how well they had played American soccer?

Had those gentlemen nearby, who had played American soccer on cinder-covered fields, with steel-toed boots, in driving rain and swirling snow, heard what she said?

If they had, shouldn't one of them have stood up and shouted, "Not kickball, lady! Not at all! The best American soccer never has been kickball, lady, don't you know that?"

Nobody stood up to say anything.

"What's that? Kickball?" hung heavily in the air.

The yeller was too surprised to reply. All he could say, lamely, was "No. American soccer's a lot better than this."

He addressed the crowd of faces that were staring at him, curious, jaws momentarily refraining from chewing. He did not know where the woman was.

"No," was all he could say, again. "Not kickball." He even turned red. He felt a little like a drunk who had instantly sobered up to find spittle and beer on his chin.

For the rest of the game, he kept on trying to cheer, but without real enthusiasm. The game slowed down again. They never played American soccer at all.

As he drove home that night, the yeller still had no idea what he should have said. In the darkness of the highway, he shook his head and chuckled helplessly. Even then, he felt some embarrassment.

He had given a wimpy answer that had none of the simple power of that lady's question, a question that hammered at the pride of American soccer.

It did no good to think that the soccer mother really meant to say, "Look, loudmouth, these young men out there so carefully passing that ball back and forth, and we polite fans here, sitting and munching Crackerjacks, know what good soccer is.

"You, however, are probably some gym teacher—or worse, you played in the old days, kicking and running and knocking each other down. American soccer, as you mean it, is past history, trash, worthless. Kickball!"

In time, it all seemed like a dream to the yeller. Had someone really been there, or was that voice just in his imagination? Was some spook haunting him after all these years of playing, watching, coaching and defending American soccer?

Was some soccer-bashing, taunting spook saying that nobody, not even soccer-lovers, ever will believe that American soccer has been anything more than kickball?

Arrgh!

Lady, maybe I was out of place, yelling at those men while everyone else was being so polite. But I wanted to make you and the players and everybody else in the stands realize that the best American soccer is as good as anybody's soccer and has been for six or seven generations! You can look it up! Better yet, ask those hall-of-famers, who went head-to-head with top foreign players.

No, the best American soccer is certainly not kickball. It's fast and it's honest, and it's never pretend. The players and the fans love the game too much. Lady, voice of the spook, if only I could tell you. . . .

Thirty-two Panels

HENRY GREGORY

It's no more than thirty-two pentagonal and hexagonal panels of leather, and several yards of stitching. It's filled only with air. Yet within each soccer ball live all who have played the game. We know who they are. Their legacy thrives in every ball, in every ball's ability to perform as it did at the feet of the masters.

Every brush has the potential to paint as it did in the hand of DaVinci.

The shots, the passes, the goals, and the saves, each can be recreated by anyone. It is only for a player to perform: to feel the ecstasy of the goal, the willpower of the slide tackle, the precision of the pass. It is for us to feel the spirit of the legacy, to see it across our eyes, across our feet, and in doing so, put our own name inside the thirty-two panels.

PART III

COACH

November:
Coach Cuts Down the Nets

CHARLES T. SHAW

The truths of philosophy I always felt pulsing in my blood. The ideas of things! I recall my first experience of being (I would learn to call it): a spigot running at the side of my house to which I listened raptly, devoutly; and my first experience of number: the collecting of stamps. The idea of shapes! We are wedded to them. From them we fashion love, beauty, work. The raker of leaves or marker of student papers attests to this. Here it is November again, and I am reminded of nature's abhorrence of permanence. My smart soccer field, for example, has been reclaimed by many-hued grasses, geese overhead in an azure sky.

I insist on playing a human part in this ritual. I cut down the nets. I am the "go to" guy now. I cut myself, too. I cut my hands. First a little nick. The field gets colder and darker than I remember. Then I begin to filet myself. I am in the presence of the source and the terminus. It purifies. No metaphors here. The ball performs the great translation, the disappearance. The goal swallows and refuses to return its . . . what? . . . prize? victim? champion?

After games players pull off uniforms. One returns to a car, air-freshener tree hanging from rearview mirror. Another becomes immersed in a crime story. Another listens to awful music. Remaining only are these goals, the suggestion of a field, a kind of joke. Like a toy left out on the lawn overnight. Or a shotup road sign out in the middle of nowhere.

73

Birth of a Team

S. S. HANNA

On a rainy Western Pennsylvania afternoon in late May, I sat in one of those wooden Siamese benches, the kind where opposing buttocks share a backboard, sipped brown water (the restaurant called it coffee), tapped my fingers on a styrofoam cup, and reflected on how rejection letters had led to a head coaching job in soccer at the college level. If anyone ever asked me how to get a soccer coaching job, I'd say, "Easy: write two hundred letters— the quirkier the better—searching for a job to teach English and coach baseball. That'll get you the head soccer job."

Coaching soccer had never interested me even though I had played the sport at the club level. While growing up in Milwaukee in the fifties, I loved baseball, played it in high school, and coached it on the organized playground leagues of the city. In college, I earned a varsity letter in football as the team's kicking specialist, kicking field goals and extra points in a manner that *The Milwaukee Journal* once noted in a feature article (with picture) to be not soccer style, not straight ahead style, "but unorthodox, like a kid taking a swipe at a tin can."

In graduate school, I lost interest in athletics and immersed myself in studying for a Ph.D. in literature. The job market for Ph.D.'s in the early seventies was horrible, and I found myself

74

drifting from one non-tenure-track teaching position to another, searching for a salary, an identity, and a sense of purpose.

Tension governed my first year at Geneva College in Beaver Falls, Pennsylvania, home of the Golden Tornadoes. I expected to be cut instantly, a casualty of declining enrollment. I wasn't. The president, instead, cut himself. Following his resignation, an interim president came, and he kept me on for another year. But the tension remained. I had to start looking for another job. It was then that I turned to the idea of coaching—not football, as I had done at a small school in Kansas, and not soccer, for I knew little about coaching that sport—but baseball, the sport that I had played and coached in Milwaukee, the sport that I had come to enjoy while watching the Milwaukee Braves rise to the status of World Champions, a team that featured Hank Aaron, Eddie Mathews, Warren Spahn, Del Crandal, Lew Burdette, Joe Adcock, Billy Bruton, Wes Covington, and other stars of years past. To us kids who grew up in Milwaukee in the fifties, the Braves were our "boys of summer."

I knew that locating a head baseball coaching job at the college level was going to be difficult enough, but to locate one where I could teach English part-time and coach baseball full-time would be even more difficult, not as difficult perhaps as locating the sister of the Unknown Soldier, but close to that. Still, I tried, and I tried hard. I ruled out the universities with major sports programs and the colleges that wished they had such programs. I telephoned a friend of mine who served as head baseball coach at a small liberal arts college in Tennessee and asked him about places that list baseball coaching vacancies for small colleges. He told me that he did not know of any, for he believed that most baseball jobs, like cheap apartments in the student ghettoes of major universities, seldom get advertised: they get passed on to friends or friends of friends. "Your best bet," my friend told me, "is to write the academic deans or vice presidents of small colleges and let them know of your intentions. If I were you, I wouldn't fool with the lowly athletic directors; go right to the top, the presidents, if need be."

That seemed like sound advice in that the dual appointment I was seeking would have to be initiated and coordinated by the chief academic officer at the college. I prepared a one-page vita that listed my academic and athletic experience and my list of publications, which by then was getting fairly lengthy.

After reproducing two hundred copies of my vita, I entered into the word processor a one-page cover letter, which proposed the idea of hiring me as head baseball coach and English-teacher-writer, one who would write a nonfiction book on the baseball program under my leadership. The proposed idea would bring "national attention to your college not via an article in a magazine or a story on the wire services or even a chapter in a book, but via an entire book devoted to your college and especially its baseball program." I concluded the letter by writing, "Now remember, if your college has been championing a losing tradition, so much the better. Indeed, I promise to do all I can to preserve that tradition which, parenthetically, might inject the book with its essential charm."

Before printing the letter, I acquired a copy of the Higher Education Directory, a work that lists the names and addresses of the main administrators of accredited institutions, isolated the names of the chief academic officers or presidents of two hundred small colleges located throughout the country, and typed those names and addresses on envelopes. That done, I printed out the cover letter for each administrator.

In time, I ended up using all two hundred vitas, spending fifty dollars in postage, and laughing at some curious and amusing responses to my cover letter, my quirky cover letter, as it might have appeared to some administrators.

The avalanche of baseball-English rejection letters began to pour in. The two hundred letters harvested 160 rejections. For the most part, the colleges with Phi Beta Kappa chapters responded in a more encouraging and receptive manner than the colleges struggling to maintain their regional accreditation.

In the Geneva mailroom, I would frequently meet the Vice President for Development, who is also the person in charge of athletics. He would be there waiting for lucrative checks from donors to a fundraising project, and I would be there waiting for rejections, which came in with disturbing faithfulness. When the Vice President took note of my prosperity, I explained to him my odd baseball-English proposal.

Sometime in mid-May when most of Geneva's students were preparing to take their final examinations and go home for the summer, the Vice President called and asked, "Are you still looking for that coaching job?"

"Sure am," I said.

"We now have one in—"

"Baseball?"

"No, no, Joe isn't leaving as far as I know," he said, referring to the head baseball coach.

"What sport?"

"Soccer." He added quickly, "But not men's."

A pause followed. Then he spoke again. "We're planning to start a women's soccer team and compete at the varsity level come September. What do you think? Are you up to it?"

"Well, you know, I played and coached football in college, I also played soccer, but I know little about coaching it. I could learn, I suppose. Let me think about it, talk to my wife and kids about it, and I'll get back to you in a week's time."

"And, by the way," he said before concluding the conversation, "you'll get a little extra pay for coaching. And I assume we'll get a book written about our soccer program."

Soon I got a letter from the Vice President. I took it home and, at dinner, shared its contents with my wife and four children. To really impress the children I converted the extra pay to Italian liras. They liked the sound of it. "Go for it, Dad."

"Let's face it," my wife said, "you're not in teaching at a small college like this one for the money."

As I was washing dishes that night, all sorts of questions competed for my attention. What could I do to make Geneva's soccer program an enjoyable experience for the players, for my family, and myself? How could I make the program different from other athletic programs that I had participated in or known? To make a program fun, I thought to myself, a coach must have control, creative control, as it were. I felt fortunate in being the head coach of the program. I expected to unfurl my own vision for the soccer program, to experience, innovate, take risks. Being the only coach, I expected to take full responsibility for the program's quirks and failures.

And what about the book? A book would have to come from this, according to my original intent. Getting soccer was a blessing in disguise. There were lots of books about baseball, but how many about soccer?

And who were going to be the team members? How many would come out for soccer? What would they be like? Will I relate to them? Will they enjoy a program coached not by a physical education instructor but by a creative writing professor? They would enjoy the program, I decided, if they all participated in all the contests, contributing to the losses or the wins, seeing their skills grow and develop. As a coach, I expected to do just that: to integrate all of them in the games regardless of their physical talents; I expected, moreover, to integrate them in a meaningful way and not simply to shove them in for a token appearance, a quick "hello-goodby" appearance that parents or fans might miss if they happened to sneak a look into their popcorn bags to see what kernels might have remained with the pallets at the bottom.

As I continued to soap and scrub those dishes, our schedule flashed into my mind. We would have several road trips, two of which were at nationally known schools: Oberlin College and Slippery Rock University, known for different reasons, I presumed. I thought it might be fun—and refreshing—if I, as a coach, did more than simply drive the players to the site of a game, coach them during the contest, and drive them back. I thought it might be fun to do some research on the away schools and to share that research with the team members before embarking on the road trips. Such an approach might enhance their educational experience, leading them to learn more than soccer skills. Many coaches of big time sports programs that I had read about often treated their athletes merely as folks with physical skills. But I wanted to treat Geneva's women soccer players as complex human beings; sensitive, thoughtful, curious, emotional, beset by fears, fraught with hopes, eager to learn.

Many coaches, my thoughts also noted, have a tendency to be lemon-sucking, rules-conscious disciplinarians, and even though their players spend a lot of time with them on the field and in the locker room, the coaches still end up projecting a one-dimensional appearance to their players. In trying to make Geneva's soccer program fun, I felt it might be wise to be loose and flexible in my leadership style. I wanted to avoid the tyranny of rigid rules; I wanted to laugh with the players, to invite them to laugh with me and even at me, to help them connect with the wit and irony of a lot of situations that we were likely to encounter during the season.

Many athletic programs that I had known featured a motivational slogan that was used throughout the season. As I neared the end of my dishwashing task, I found myself mentally flipping through a lot of slogans, searching for one that might be appropriate for our program. I concluded that rather than have a slogan for the season, it might be fun to devise a slogan or a theme for a given week of practice leading up to a game or for select games.

Now I was on the knives and forks and spoons. The words of a small college football coach from Arizona navigated my mind. "My wife becomes a widow with the kids during football season," he said. I vowed to avoid that trap. Indeed, I thought it would be fun to involve my wife and children as much as possible in my coaching activities. My wife, a registered nurse, could help with injuries, with taping ankles, and similar concerns, especially on game day. The children, I thought, could occasionally come to practice and the home games; they could help with ball retrieval, supply the players with drinks, position the cones on the field, tease and be teased.

The dishes were done. I told my wife about some of my thoughts. The responsibilities of coaching and traveling and losing had begun to settle into my thoughts. "What fun," the nurse said. "You're going to be the midwife of the women's soccer program."

Afterword

"Coach," Angi said as she stood in my office. "I'll sum up our season for you in the words of an old expression."
"And what would that be?" I asked.
She looked around my L-shaped, book-lined office, stared at a picture of James Joyce that along with those of other writers decorated a wall, then spoke in a slow and distinct manner: "It was all a crock of—"
"Oh, please, Angi, please, don't say it."
"But it's not what you're thinking, coach."
I looked at her, dressed in jeans patched with the anti-war symbol of the late sixties, the era of her birth, and said, "Okay, go ahead, complete the expression."
"Our season," she said, paused, smiled, then added, "was a crock of wit."
Angi occasionally acted in unusual and unpredictable ways. I always feared—hoped—that one day on a soccer road trip, she might turn around in the bucket seat in the front of the van, call the players to attention, whip out a copy of *Howl* and begin reading. And if I knew Angi, she would first read the last line of William Carlos Williams' Introduction to *Howl* where Williams says, "Hold back the edges of your gowns, Ladies, we are going through hell."
"It *was* a crock, wasn't it?" I smiled and glanced at the caterpillar below the nose of John Steinbeck. He surely could have grown a better looking moustache than that, I thought, turned to Angi, and said, "Sure we had our problems, but we had a lot of fun, too, didn't we?"
"We did, and I hope you capture that fun—or at least a bit of it—in the book you're going to write."

Volunteer Coach of the Pink Pumas

B. W. Bales

Part 1

It was the hottest day of August, and we were down by the banks of the bone-dry riverbed. My son was next in line to be registered at the innocent age of ten. It was years ago, but I still remember the words of the soccer commissioner: "If you want a soccer team, you're going to need a soccer coach."

Sweat dripped down the faces of the mothers and fathers in line. Suddenly we'd all become dentist-office quiet, as together we watched the ants crawl around at our feet.

We had two things in common that day that brought us into the dustbowl of a soccer field. We all had ten-year-old future World Cup players who needed only slight direction in order to pave the road to stardom. And we were all the bottom of the barrel, undeniable scum of the earth, low-life LATE REGISTRANTS!!!

I naturally assumed that the others had perfectly reasonable alibis for their tardiness in registering. After all, the season was to begin in two weeks. I figured most had either just moved to the area, or perhaps had just recently gotten around to reading the notice on the bulletin board at the local Mom & Pop store. It didn't occur to me that maybe, like myself, they hadn't had the money at the time of the first registration.

The soccer commissioner didn't care one way or the other. "No coach, no team!" he said.

We looked at each other, pleading silently. After eternity passed, a petite Hispanic woman took a solemn step out from the line.

"I will help with coach. But I don' know much of the game," she said shyly.

Everyone seemed pleased that someone had volunteered to do something, though we weren't quite sure what she had volunteered to do. We supposed it was a start.

Behind me was a hefty blond woman jabbing her husband's shoulder and saying, "You can do it, Clint. Tell them you'll do it."

Clint didn't budge. His size fifteen feet were planted solidly in the dust. He stood tall and lean with a Stetson perched atop his brown wavy hair. Arms folded, he continued to chew on a wad of tobacco, ignoring his wife's pleas.

In scanning the adults, I could see that they had come from all walks of life. The cattle ranches, the factories, the board rooms and the barrios were all represented. We were all together on the desolate ground to watch our miniature Pelés chase a ball up and down a field. I wished I had managed my money a little better. My son and I could have been on a nice, grassy field next to a well-kept elementary school on a cool spring morning. They would have already had coaches there, true and wise volunteers who would give freely of their time in order to mold our children into a championship team.

I looked up and down the line of children. What a crew! These guys would be the Bad News Bears of soccer. Clint Jr. wore a striking pair of bib overalls with one leg rolled up to just below the knee. The other pant leg completely covered his left shoe, if in fact he was wearing a shoe on that foot.

The daughter of the petite Hispanic woman was modeling a well-worn pair of denim shorts and a stained t-shirt that read "CON PEPSI, NO HAY SED." She was a pretty little girl with long, shiny black hair and black eyes. Her tennis shoes were laced with neon pink strings.

One kid at the end of the line had been even later than the rest of us. He was the epitome of preppiness. He looked as if he had walked right out of an elite soccer rag advertisement. He sported two-toned Umbro shorts, a blue and white pinstriped keeper's shirt, Lotto Italia shoes, one blue sock and one white, and . . . and . . . KEEPER GLOVES??? In this 120-degree heat? Weird, but perhaps he was a blessing. At least the team would have an experienced goalkeeper.

I surveyed the line more intently now, looking for others who could help make this a viable team. There was the two-footer. (This is not a reference to his ability to kick equally with both feet, but to his height.) There was the loud mouth know-it-all. There was the bully who was pushing the two-footer. There was the space cadet who was fifty meters downfield, pretending to be a fighter pilot over the Persian Gulf. And there was the loner, who was propped up by a dead tree stump calculating the spread of the hole in the ozone.

What a lost cause this bunch is, I thought. I couldn't believe it. I grinned. I coughed. I kicked up some dirt. I squirmed.

"Okay, I'll coach."

My words came quickly. I was startled. Did I say that out loud? I saw a line of relieved faces. Yes, I had said it out loud.

The commissioner went to work checking birth certificates and collecting rolled coins and checks. My son, hands in pockets, shuffled over to me. I knew he'd be overwhelmed with pride and joy that his ol' man had gotten into the community spirit and agreed to coach his team.

"Whatya do that for, Dad?" he asked.

It was going to be a very long season.

Part 2

After I'd volunteered to coach the team, my son and I returned home to tell the understanding, loving, and supportive one to whom I vowed never to shoot to the near post or cross the ball in front of our own goal. I knew she'd see the need for the players to have an experienced, knowledgeable soccer coach.

"But you don't know anything about soccer," she said. "You aren't even working full time, and you're going to be out on a soccer field every night?" she slide tackled. I knew better than to say that it wouldn't take up EVERY night.

Taking out a pen and paper to jot down some soccer notes, I started thinking, and then I thought some more. After about ten minutes of thought, I realized that I didn't have anything to jot. I didn't know anything about the game. Though my son, Barton, had played for two seasons, I had always been content to yell from the touch line with the other parents. I'd cheer for Barton and his teammates. I learned to bellow, "Offside!" if the other team got a breakaway, and "Trip!" if one of OUR players fell down. And naturally I had my standard digs for the refs and linesmen, such as, "Did you leave your glasses at home?" and "If you weren't so fat, you could keep up with the game." That was pretty much my soccer lingo. I was in serious trouble.

At that moment the phone rang. John, the commissioner, was on the other end. He explained that the other teams in the league had already taken all the practice times for the fields at the elementary school, but I was free to use Fallout Field, where our registration had been held. Nobody else was going to use it, so I could conduct my practices any days and times I wished.

"Thanks," I said.

I woke early the next day, determined to expand my knowledge of soccer. I went to the library. I went to the city to take out a second mortgage on the house so I could purchase a few items at the soccer shop.

Upon returning home, I had Bart assist me in unloading the car. He suggested we take inventory. We hauled in twelve soccer books, thirty-two small orange cones, a whistle, a ball, an air pump, a first-aid kit and a water jug. This was going to be a great season.

I was pumped and ready to get started, but after reading a chapter from the first book about runs and overlaps, I came to a startling realization: I didn't know what any of it meant.

Maybe I'd have better luck with video tapes. Wow! I sat for hours, absorbed in watching fifteen billion of the greatest goals ever scored, highlights of every World Cup since 1958, and something about Diego Maradona's magic hand. Now this was good stuff. My team would be executing overhead kicks from mid-field, finishing with diving headers, and bending balls into the net from the corners. We were going to be awesome! I was sure my guys could do that stuff. I'd just have to figure out how to teach it.

Knowing our first practice was only a day away, I crammed all the information I could from the books and videos. Then I went *in cognito* to the elementary field to see what the other coaches were doing at their practices. But nothing, no books, videos or spying could have prepared me for that first practice.

It was the second hottest day of August. I gave Bart an assist for helping to get things organized at the field. We had gotten there a little early to prep for practice. In placing the cones on the field, we kicked up the dust into a choking haze. The goals were made of wood, but one was missing a post and a crossbar. There were no lines marked. But we were ready. We had placed cones to dribble around. We had cones ready to pass through. And we had cones set to shoot from behind.

We waited. Nobody came. We waited longer. Still, nobody. Finally Bart asked what time it was.

"Four thirty," I replied.

"But practice doesn't start until 5:30, Dad."

"Okay, so we came a little early," I conceded.

At precisely 5:31 the cars and trucks began rolling into the lot. Kids jumped out and sprinted down to the field. They were obviously anxious to get down to some serious soccer. As they came onto the field, I lined them up facing me. They looked determined. Sure, they didn't wear soccer gear. True, they didn't have soccer shoes. And, as I viewed the line, I saw what else they didn't have. Soccer balls!!!

"Why didn't ya'll bring soccer balls?" I questioned.

"I don't have one," they shouted.

As I prepared to call roll, a shiny new Lexus pulled up. Carlton, the preppie, leaped from the car before it had even stopped. He ran full tilt down the barren slope toward the field. Just as he neared the bottom, he tripped over his untied laces and completed three somersaults in the dirt before coming to rest. We stood silently, waiting to see if Carlton would recover from the humiliating performance. He rose and walked toward us, a blood smear across his knee and a trickle of red from his mouth.

"Are you okay, Carlton?" I asked as he closed ranks with the others.

Fighting back tears, he sniffled softly, "I tore my Umbros and soiled my shirt."

Oh, no. It was bad enough that my first player injury had happened BEFORE my first practice; but worse yet, my goalkeeper obviously didn't like to get dirty. On the brighter side, however, his father rolled a brand new, hand-stitched, fully inflated, one-year-guaranteed soccer ball down the hill and onto the field. Now we had TWO soccer balls!

After directing Carlton to the first-aid kit, I started down the roster. I remembered some of the players from registration.

"Barton Stone," I called in an authoritative tone.

"You know I'm here, Dad. You brought me."

"Carlton Fairbanks III?"

"Present."

"Alicia Flores, are you here?"

I knew she was, of course. I just didn't want to draw attention to the fact that she was the only girl.

"Aquí," she answered quietly.

"Harley Holmes?" I waited. "Harley Holmes?"

Everyone looked up and down the line, but no one replied. Then I spotted somebody shinnying up a tree along the river bank. Oh yes, I thought to myself. The airhead.

"Okay. We'll bring him over when we're ready to get started." I looked around. "Clint Johnson, Jr.?" I continued.

"Here, sir."

"Hey, I like those bibs, Clint."

"Thank you, sir. And all my friends call me Bear."

"Well, since we're your friends, we'll call you Bear, too. Adam, quit pushing! I won't have anyone on my team pushing teammates. You got that, Mister?"

"But he was in my way. I didn't do anything."

"Roberto Salas?"

"I'm over here, behind Bear."

Oh yeah. The two-footer.

"Rodney?"

"Yo, Coach. And I want to be center forward 'cause I'm the best player here."

"Well, if you are, Rodney, I want you to know that I always keep my best player on the bench so we don't expose our strength to the other teams."

"Mark?"

"Here."

"Harazi?"

"Yep," replied Harazi, grinning from ear to ear.

"Nice to have you aboard, Harazi. Have you ever played before?"

"Yep. When I lived in Saudi Arabia."

I liked the sound of that.

"Clifford?"

"It's just Cliff, Coach."

"Okay, I'll make a note of that."

"First, we are going to have to think of a name for our team," I explained.

"Falcons."

"Jets."

"Raiders."

"Cowboys."

"Broncos."

"Wait. Wait. One at a time. And remember this is a SOCCER team, not a football team."

This is crazy. They have been here for twenty minutes, and we haven't done anything.

"Alicia, what would you like to name the team?" I inquired.

"My favorite team in Mexico is the PUMAS."

"PUMAS it is!" I said.

So, it wasn't my first choice, but what's in a name? I just wanted to move on.

The remainder of practice went as well as could be expected. The players got to know each other a little, and I was able to use my keen observation skills to detect some of their strengths. I jotted down some of the more noticeable qualities.

Clinton Jr.:	Big, fast, strong foot—sweeper
Alicia:	Good speed, handles ball—forward
Bart:	Strong foot, good passer—center half
Harley:	Dribbles well, aggressive—outside half
Harazi:	Strong foot, southpaw—left fullback

When Bart and I arrived home that night, we were greeted at the door by the Sweeper to whom I promised never to foul in the penalty box, or ever leave my mark. Much to my surprise she seemed to be in a pleasant mood.

"The commissioner called," she said. "He wants you to pick up your team's uniforms."

Now she was smirking. Something is definitely wrong with this picture.

Okay, I'll make a fake run to the goal, and drive this stopper into submission.

"Oh, that's no big deal," I said. "I was planning on selling our car and buying the team some real nice uniforms."

"He just wants you to pick them up, Hon. You don't need to get sarcastic."

"Sure. Now what's the real story?"

"Nothing, nothing at all. They did only have one set of uniforms left, though. And they're pink."

"Pink?"

Bart's head dropped.

"Great, Dad. Now we're the PINK PUMAS."

"What's in a color?" I said, hoping they weren't going to issue a coach's shirt.

PART IV

ON THE FIELD

Soccer Dreams

DAVID UPDIKE

When I was a senior in college I did something that, even now, fifteen years later pains me in memory: I quit the soccer team. It was not so much the quitting that still bothers me, but the way that I did it.

It was the third or fourth day of preseason training camp, at a small prep school in Rhode Island—a beautiful late summer day, the sun shining and the grass wet with dew, and we were in the middle of our morning session when, under some long forgotten pretext, I jogged to our dormitory, changed into my street clothes, scribbled a note to my coach, packed my bag, walked quickly down the tree-lined drive to the street, and hitchhiked back to Boston. When I got there, finally, I was still in a daze with the enormity of what I had just done, and ducked into a bar for a beer, to collect myself, and when I got back to campus I lay down under a tree in the gathering dusk, staring up through the branches, wondering why I had just done what I'd done.

I had been on the team the year before, and the year before that, and this, my final season, was to be the pinnacle of my soccer career. Although I had never "started" consistently, I had played a lot as a junior and had trained hard that summer to get in shape; but when I'd gotten to preseason camp, all of my hopes seemed to fade under the dull familiarity of it all, and the gathering sense that, no matter what I did, no matter how hard I tried, my role on the team was fixed, predetermined, and would not change. I was a forward back then, and there were a couple of players ahead of me with more extravagant talents than my own. In practice, they were scoring lots of goals, and I remember feeling that, no matter what I did, I would always be behind them and never really be a part of the team. It was not that I didn't love the sport anymore: it was that I loved it too much, and could not sit idly by as it became something I did not want—a kind of drudgery, with no sense of possiblility, no sense that, through perseverance and hard work and desire, I could elevate myself in the eyes of our coach and become the player I always thought I should become. This, it seems to me now, is the most important thing for any athlete, or person, for that matter: a sense of potential upward mobility and a feeling that you can rise up through your own limitations and reach a higher level. My coach, somehow, had not given me this feeling, and instead I felt my role on the team had calcified, and, with the intuitive clarity of youth, felt that this would not change, and with an impetuosity I have often regretted since, I quit the team, and thus ended my collegiate soccer career.

Until then, soccer had been the sustaining passion of my life. When I was twelve, my family lived in England for a year, and there I discovered that, what baseball and football didn't do for me, soccer did—the big green fields, the sense of near-nakedness and freedom, the absence of some short-haired, baseball-hatted coach, bellowing at me from the sidelines. This was a players' game, and I became addicted to its varied sensations—the wet grass; the low scuttling clouds drifting like battleships over England's bright green fields; the ball bouncing, with a satisfying whomp, off the crown of my forehead; the sensation of receding foes, whom I had just dribbled past, drifting behind me like frozen statues; and the way things seemed to slow down, when, ball at my feet, I approached the goal, and the unearthly euphoria I felt when I scored, ball moving slowly past a lumbering, distended goaltender.

But when I got back to America, after a year away, I discovered that my town had no organized youth programs, and that my friends did not entirely share my rabid enthusiasm, and the soccer I played was limited to summer pickup games, and the ten or eleven games a year I played for junior high and then the high school team. I practiced by myself, mostly, in my yard, where I constructed a soccer net, and coaxed my reluctant, immediate relatives to play with me.

If I had lived in Europe, I would have been playing thirty or forty games a year, and by the time I got out of college, would have been a considerably better player. Instead, I was high on potential and energy, low in savvy and composure and experience.

In truth, I had always liked my college coach. A short, barrel-chested Englishman with a shock of reddish, brownish hair, prone to lusty pronouncements like "bloody hell!" and "a damn lackluster performance!" When he wasn't coaching, George was a teacher of sixth-grade math students, and I suspect he might have been better with kids than volatile, high-strung Harvard students, in search of their egos and identities. He tended to overcoach and attempt last-minute tactical maneuvers that worked against the best interests of the team, like starting a player at a position he had never played before in practice. He was not a great motivator, and for many players their freshman year was their best. But he liked to joke, and laugh, have cups of tea after the games, and he came to some of our post game parties and didn't complain when suspicious clouds of smoke came billowing out of the back room.

In any event, I was a senior and had played under George for two years, and quitting the team was a kind of betrayal. We had always had a certain, unspoken rapport, and for two summers he had invited me to coach at a soccer camp he ran in New Hampshire. The year I quit, they had a bad season; two or three years later he lost his job, allegedly after taking a team on a tour of England, getting in a fight with his brother after a game, and then, somehow, leaving the team to fend for itself for several days while he sorted out his troubles. Within four or five years after he left, the new Harvard coach took the team to the NCAA final four.

I, meanwhile, was living in New York, trying to be a grownup, and also playing soccer, trying to make peace with a clouded soccer past. I played in Brooklyn, on the reserve team of a semi-professional team associated with an Italian Social Club and bankrolled by a Brooklyn car dealership titan with rumored links to the underworld. I was on the first team for a while, but this involved watching most of the games from the bench, though I did play one entire game once, and we won, 1–0. Afterwards, back in the social club, someone slipped me a check for twenty-five dollars, but by the next game I was back to being an amateur. This was a kind of soccer world entirely new to me: the Cosmopolitan League is one of the oldest in the country. Almost all the teams had a strong ethnic base: Greek, Italian, German, Croatian. They played on scrappy, bumpy, rocky fields in New Jersey, Brooklyn, Long Island, but the players—most of them recent immigrants from Europe, South America, the Caribbean—played with a fluency and skill I was not familiar with. I practiced by myself in cement playgrounds, played with Rastafarians in Washington Square Park, and then, going nowhere, quit the Italians and joined the Croatians, who had advertised for players in the weekly soccer newspaper. They practiced on Randalls Island, in the middle of the East River, and to get there I had to take the subway to 125th Street, in Harlem, and walk across the Triborough Bridge. They played their games out in New Jersey, on a piece of land by a lake owned by a Croatian Church and called, predictably, Croatialand. I had three happy years on this team, and in my final year we won the League Championship, and "The Cup." More importantly, perhaps, I had learned how to play, and felt I had reached my potential and no longer thought much about how I had quit my college team. I had put that old demon to rest.

When I moved back to Boston, I played in a Harvard Alumni game, and there ran into some of my old teammates. Together we formed a team and joined a local soccer league. This, too, was fun, playing with old friends, against worse teams, mostly, and even scrimmaging the Harvard Varsity, or J.V., now and then. We rose up through the ranks, won the second division our first year, and in our second came in third in the first division. And then, in our third year, everything came together: a new goalie, a few new players, among them, a Harvard law student who played professionally in the off-season; and the Harvard coach, who had been a part of a national championship team at Indiana.

In the second half of the season, a friend and I assumed managerial control of the team and continued our climb to glory. By late October, we had already won the league and were working our way through the Cup—a single elimination tournament played between all the teams in the league: to win both, in soccer parlance, is called the "double."

My own life, by this time, was rather busy: I had two or three teaching jobs and was married, and my wife was pregnant, expecting a child in the middle of November; as my team worked its way though the opponents in the Cup, it occurred to me that the birth of my son was on a collision course with the projected date for the Cup final. And sure enough, we made it to the semifinal, and then the final, which was scheduled a day or two after my wife's due date. "It's all right," I jested. "If there's a conflict, I'll be there immediately after the game." No laugh. It was a busy time.

I continued to attend birthing classes and worked out the details for the Cup final. The Harvard Varsity season was over and, because the coach was one of our players, we were granted permission to use the Harvard Varsity field—the scene of my bittersweet soccer experience and unfulfilled dreams of glory.

The week before the game, or the birth, or both, I was nervous, apprehensive, on edge. My wife was doing well, showing no signs of going into labor, and the weather report for game day was favorable—overcast with a slight chance of showers. I was conscious my life was about to change dramatically, but I did not know how, other than that a demanding person would soon be moving into our house. The morning of the game, all was still well and my wife gave me the go-ahead. "Nothing's going to happen today," she said. "You should play."

I hurried toward the field, arriving early, as usual—a half an hour before anyone else—and took a few shots, while the low, gray English-looking clouds drifted overhead. But I was still nervous, tight, and I kept half-missing the shots, and they all went just wide of the post. My teammates began to arrive, and then the other team, but by game time, there was no sign of a referee. "Who was supposed to call the ref?" someone asked, and with a sudden flush of terror, I wondered if it should have been me. But no—this was the Cup final—the league should have taken care of it.

"Look over there," one of my teammates said, pointing across the field to the bleachers where a lone figure sat, huddling in the cold. "Who do you think that is?" he asked.

I knew instinctively: the unmistakable shape of my old coach, huddling in the cold. "I called him and told him we were playing here," my friend said.

We waved him over and exchanged greetings, hoping he had forgotten about my quitting the team a decade or so before. Probably not, but he seemed to harbor no ill feelings and, as he had left Harvard under shadowy circumstances himself, I felt we were on equal footing, somehow. He looked none the worse for the intervening decade, short and handsome and windswept, jocular and with a certain, subdued charisma, making jokes and telling stories, showing an avuncular interest in his old players. But still, there was no referee, and someone half-facetiously suggested George referee the game. "I would, if I had decent footware," he said, pointing down to his shiny leather shoes, recently polished. Shoes of his size were procured, we negotiated with the other team, and it was agreed that he could ref the game, at least until the real ref showed up.

And so we played—my former teammates and I on one side, and on the other, the unlikely combination of Iranian and Haitian players. In urban soccer leagues in America, any combination is possible. They were good, and the field was big and green and smooth, a vast improvement over the small, stony patches of overused earth we usually played on. The wind died down, clouds gave way to patches of blue, and ten or fifteen minutes into the game I received a pass near the top of the penalty box. I faked a pass, took a shot, and mis-hit it, as I had my practice shots before the game. But this time, something happened that had never happened in college: the shot was not too hard, but low, and perfectly, if accidentally, placed, and as the goalie fell like a tree, a second too late, it nipped into the corner of the net. 1–0.

But the other team was persistent, and a minute from the end of the half one of their players took a long, looping shot that spun just out of reach of our goalie, hit the inside of the post, and bounced in.

At the half, our old coach-turned-ref, gave us all an unexpected, animated pep talk. "You're making mincemeat of them on the left side, lads. Just keep it up, keep it on the ground, nice short passes. Try to move it through midfield and cross it into the box before the defense closes down on you. But keep it on the ground. You can beat these guys all day long." He was happy, it was clear, animated and alive. We were his boys again, and his advice seemed sound.

"Let's go, fellows," he said, blowing the whistle for the second half. "I don't have all day, you know."

In the second half, our opponents had the wind, and both teams were playing well and hard, and I remember being conscious, at some point, of simply being happy to be playing on this late fall day, in the wind, on this big green field, while my wife prepared to give birth. I was not enormously worried about who won—though it would be more fun, of course, if we did. And then, ten or so minutes to the end of the game, it happened. One of our players had the ball down on the left side, near the corner, trying to get enough room for a cross. I was on the right, at midfield, and I kept thinking the ball would go out of bounds, but it didn't and I was drifting in toward the goal when, in a flurry of activity, my teammate beat one man, then another; the ball bounced around between their shins, hopped up once before him, and he lofted a soft gentle cross in front of the net—too far out for the goalie, but not too far for me. I saw it all the way, and sprinted into the space where the ball was softly falling, like a snowflake, and there, the unsuspecting orb and my on-rushing forehead converged at the same, exact instant, at the same, happy place in the universe, with the pleasant, inevitable result: the ball flying, at high velocity, into the back, lefthand side of the net. I did not so much see it, as feel it, and without breaking stride I wheeled around, arms upraised sprinting back up the field through the blurry shapes of my teammates as they converged around me, the sound of the wind rushing past my ears.

After that, the other team was emotionally defeated, a vivid illustration of the wind gone out of someone's sails, and a minute or two from the end, we scored again. They pleaded offsides, but feebly, and we all knew it was over. During those final minutes of the game, as we all ran around somewhat aimlessly in the giddy understanding that we were going to win, my old coach made a quip that I should have scored three goals, not just two, and then blew the final whistle. Afterwards, he changed his shoes, hung around for a while in the glow of our collective euphoria, had a beer, and then headed off. Everyone agreed, including the other team, that he had been a fair and excellent referee and had saved the game. My ony regret is that he didn't make it, somehow, into the post-game photo of the team.

A day or two later, my son was born in good health, nine pounds ten ounces, and a new phase of my life began. The weather turned suddenly, bitterly cold. Autumn was over and winter had begun. The following season, our team began a slow decline brought on by injuries, babies, the encroaching demands of families and careers.

Two or three years after that, I learned that my old coach had passed away, unexpectedly, back in his native England, collapsing, we were told, onto his plate of food during lunch, after spending the morning playing a game of pickup soccer with some kids. It was sad, shocking, and the manner of his death sounded somewhat like the plotline of one of his own macabre jokes.

There was a memorial service at the school where he had taught, but I couldn't go and, in any case, we had already said our goodbyes and settled our own small differences. In retrospect, there was something unreal and dream-like about our final meeting: the big green field of my unfulfilled, soccer past; the low gray clouds of my childhood in England; my old coach, climbing out of the stands, out of the past, to serve as referee, unwitting accomplice to my unexpected heroics. Even my son had postponed his birth so I could fulfill my own childhood dreams: two goals, one in each half—one into each of the nets in which I never scored in college. These goals, I now see, were a gift from the soccer gods—a reward for a lifetime of devoted service. There was poetic symmetry, and a certain, circular beauty to it all, and a reassuring lesson of forgiveness and redemption. It was my greatest soccer moment and, in the middle of it all was the figure of my former coach—a short, bellicose Englishman wearing street clothes and borrowed shoes, with a thatch of reddish, brownish hair, shouting happily into the autumn wind.

Replay

JEAN HOUSTON

There is nothing more final
More dead
Than the ball in the net.
The trajectory of surprise complete,
So quickly over.
Bright agent turned blank object.
The mind reels back
Mind's eye replays the startling synaps-pass
Its tingling message stinging on mind's foot
Terse
Unrehearsed
and undeciphered—
Live with possibilities.

Out of Retirement

NANCY E. SEITZ

Two years between games was a long time for my daughter. It was also a long time for me. Neither of us expected her to play soccer again. But Courtney was called back from retirement to play just this one game for a former coach whose team was one player short for a tournament.

Many years earlier, my shy little fourth-grader with the chestnut brown hair and eyes to match had walked into the house one afternoon and announced that she wanted to play "that game."

"What game?" I asked.

"That game that Sharon plays where you kick the ball into the net. I was just watching them. It looks like fun," she said.

The next ten years of our lives—my life, hers, her father's, her two younger brothers'—were all soccer. My husband coached. My daughter played during the spring, summer, winter, fall, outdoors and indoors. Often she was the only girl on the team. She played on teams sponsored by the community, by the town, by various organizations.

From the beginning she was good. She learned quickly and she was fast. She played any position, but was most at home on the right wing. From there, deftly, she'd steal the ball from the opposing player with fancy footwork and race with it up the right sideline. She'd finish the play by putting the ball in the net—high, low, this corner, that.

Soccer was good for Courtney. It gave her recognition. It gave her the confidence that comes with knowing that you do something better than most others who do it. It demanded that she stretch the limits of her physical and psychological self, and she did. It helped her to put the needs of a group before her own needs. It taught her to work hard.

By the time she reached high school, every coach in the northern part of the state knew who she was. She tried out for the team, then waited and worried—and made it. She was the second freshman to be chosen for the women's varsity team in the history of the school. But making the team turned out to be the easy part. Gaining the acceptance of the upperclass team members was tougher. She lugged the equipment, ran for the water, and took the teasing. But when the coach put her in a game for the first time, she scored almost immediately. She was in.

For four years Courtney played for the school, for the team, for us and for herself. Through twisted ankles, exhaustion, mono, and bruises, in good weather and bad, she played soccer. Sunburned or frozen, parched or soaked, we cheered and held our breaths and cried. She was chosen best "all-league," "all-area," "all-county," all-state." Newspapers interviewed and featured her. The house became cluttered with trophies and plaques.

And through it all my daughter never lost her sense of herself, of humility. She never forgot that she was just a person with a talent and the desire and capacity to develop it. She gave back to the game of soccer as much as it had given to her. She'd help an opposing player up after a fall. She'd stay late at school to help a less adept teammate work on skills. With her brother, she coached a team of younger girls. She played hard and fair, every time. When she won, she was gracious. When she lost, she never hung her head.

* * *

In our town there are two high schools. Both have soccer teams. There is enormous rivalry between them. They do not play against each other in the regular schedule. But at the end of soccer season Courtney's senior year, her year as captain, they came up against each other for the county championship. This game was more important to the team and to my daughter than any game had ever been.

The game was played under the lights on the field of a neutral, out-of-town school. The day had been my last at a job I'd spent weeks trying to find a way not to leave. I'd said goodbye to my working partner of nine years. I had no other job to go to. I was worried about money and about my own competence. I had to dig deep down behind my own concerns to be fully present at this game, to remember what it meant to my daughter. It didn't take long.

It was chilly in the stands. The field lay in a hollow. An eerie evening mist began to descend as the girls warmed up. Under the lights, the ball acquired shadows and shapes it didn't have in daylight. The game began. Courtney scored her goals and made the right plays. She was nervous. I saw her retch once or twice at the sidelines. The coach spoke to her. She kept playing. The other team was tough. The score went back and forth. Her team dominated, but could not pull ahead. Each half seemed endless. My heart was pounding, every muscle tensed. She played harder, ran faster, covered more ground, fought exhaustion. When time ran out, the score was tied.

But a county championship game can't end in a tie. The referee called for a "sudden death" shootout. Each team had three shots on goal. One player at a time would bang away at the opposing goalie. Each team's first shooter scored. The second girl from the school across town also made her goal. Courtney approached the ball and drove it neatly into the upper left corner of the net, just beyond the goalie's reach. The third player from across town put hers in. The third, and last, player from Courtney's team missed, slamming the ball harmlessly off the upright. We had lost by one point. It was time to pack up and go home.

I was shivering uncontrollably. I sat and watched the stands empty. I saw the deserted field through the mist, the shafts of light shining down on the glistening grass, the discarded water cups, the empty goal. And I saw my daughter alone on the bench.

That evening left its mark on Courtney, and probably just as indelibly on me. She'd come to know that sometimes, no matter how hard you try or how deserving you are, things aren't always going to be all right.

So, when Courtney agreed to play again two years later, I was surprised. She'd decided not to play soccer at college. She'd taken as much from the game as she wanted and given it all she could. She was ready to move on—to academics, to other challenges, to adulthood. And so she had. Then she came back. And she played well for someone who hasn't kicked a ball in two years. For anyone, in fact. The opposition was rough, and afterwards, she was battered and bruised.

On the way home I asked what had made her decide to play today.

"Just wanted to see if I could still do it," she said. "I had to know if it had all been real, had to feel within myself that I'd been good."

"And?" I asked.

"I was. And I can still do it. But I probably won't have to again."

The Great Soccer Massacre

BRENDON FOWLER

The foot blotted out the sun, air across the blunt shoe shrieking as the foot touched down, muscles straining. The cartilage absorbed the shock of the impact, and the foot lifted, propelling the body forward. The other leg came around, pulled into a tight arc by the restrictive bone structures. The white and black ball spun slowly out of orbit, meeting the foot just below the ankle. Its energy redirected, the ball tore close to the field. Two people were there to meet it, and cleat clashed on armor as the two fought and twisted until one finally connected with the ball, sending it off again. This scene was repeated over and over, the whirling dance that was soccer following some hidden rhythm broken only by the shouts of irate spectators.

The bench unit heaved a collective sigh. Once again resigned to eighty minutes of bench riding and splinter picking, these hardy fellows resisted the urge to bolt out of the 12.56-degree weather and into the warmth of the school. The players on the field shouted and screamed, weaving for the ball. Every now and then it would roll toward one of the white-netted goals at either end, only to be kicked away by the quick defenders. The men on the bench exchanged weary glances. They'd showed team spirit. They'd come to all the practices. With a collective GPA of 99.767 they'd watched starter after starter shank shots over the net.

They'd fetched water. They'd sat on the bench listening to each other's teeth chatter.

Using their collective I.Q. of 8,793, they slowly came to the realization that this was really stupid. What talent wasted! Why, they could practically hear themselves age! Moments of important history were slipping away, as they watched their legs turn a wonderful shade of frostbite. Yet they endured, with the stoic hope that some supreme being, even mightier than the coach, might realize their plight and drop a comet onto the playing field.

Half time. The starters left the field and grasped at the water jug thoughtfully procured by one of the non-starters. These resilient folk stood up slowly to keep their joints from cracking in the cold. The group trekked to the far goal. They readied themselves for an uplifting speech or an inspirational hymn from the coach, but they were disappointed. "I haven't seen a lot of enthusiasm on the bench," spake the coach, his warm jacket pulled tight. To a single man the non-starters looked at him, unable to protest through frozen lips.

Late in the second half, an incident occurred that would be recorded in the annals of history for all time as "The Results of Messing With Very Cold People Wearing Long Cleats," or, "The Great Soccer Massacre."

It had begun to rain, and the game degenerated into a mud wrestling match. Players from each team slammed into each other, and several purple losing-limbs-while-offsides cards were distributed. After one particular pileup, a player from the opposing team was given the dreaded black good-for-one-free-decapitation card. Sputtering obscenities, this player slowly jogged around the field and passed in front of the bench. One astute bencher seized the opportunity and called out, quite clearly, "Is that your jersey number or your number of Y-chromosomes?" The player did not understand the question, but knew he had been ridiculed. He turned slowly and with effortless grace stated, "That means a lot coming from a bunch of fourth-string bench warmers." Then he casually flicked his leg towards the bench. A globule of mud detached itself from his cleat and sailed through the air. Time ceased to pass for the benchers as they watched the mud, outlined against the gray November sky, begin its descent, picking up speed and completing its arc directly on top of the bench, splattering into a wide circle. Those nearest the impact site drew back in horror. At first they had discounted the player's retort as a compliment, since they were actually *fifth* string. But to befoul their bench with damnable field mud was blasphemy. With a roar and a shout the bench surged forward, their rested legs carrying them up to and over the player, who was unaware of the force he had unleashed. Cleats pounded him flat, mud and gore covered him and the ground around him.

The group of pine riders halted, their anger checked momentarily by their new surroundings. They were on the field. A stunned hush fell over the crowd. It dawned on the referees that the home team had too many players on the field. The other team was dumbfounded, although a few heads turned to stare angrily at the carnage. Their trampled teammate broke the silence with a groan. Slowly and calmly, a bench player stepped from the group on the field, crossed to the trampled player, and swiftly lifted his foot, bringing it down on the player's bright new pair of $4,678 Patrick cleats. An angry shout filled the air from the other team's benchers as they surged onto the field.

Cleats flashed in the crisp wet cold. The teams clashed again and again, starters and benchers fighting as a team. The referees could no longer keep up with the fouls and cards, but swept imperiously into the fray. "Stop this!" they shouted, whistles screeching. It seemed as if order would be restored, and then suddenly a home-team bencher reached into his soccer bag and took out his water jug. With it he pegged a ref in the head. Many were the voices that cried, "Good throw!" and "Bravo!"

The other team was huddled by their goal. The home team set about chopping down trees behind the goal with each other and constructed a small catapult. Winding it back, they loaded it with an orange corner flag. "Shoot!" cried the lookout, perched atop the goal post. The flag rocketed down the field, well on its way to the opposite goal, but with a crunching sound it landed on the roof of the other team's bus. "Hurrah!" and "Yippee!" cried the home team, with a "Nice arc, man!" thrown in.

Time passed. Mighty empires rose and fell. The conflict raged on. The original field was scarred, its boundaries hacked and shredded by trenches dug and missiles kicked and thrown. It was difficult to tell where the grass ended and the benches began. Both teams had been whittled down through the years, even with the inclusion of many JV players for sectionals.

One day, a certain bencher looked up into the sky. The sun was coming out, and he looked at it as if he had never seen it before. The struggle was difficult, and many of his friends had been wounded and taken away. Try as he might, he could not keep his cleats clean either. Then, suddenly, the coach turned and stared at him. "Get in there," he rasped, for his vocal cords had been nearly severed by an indirect. Excitement and joy filled the player's mind, and he rushed for his gear. Donning his shin guards, he followed the winding maze of barbed wire and trenches up to the front, at center field. Along the way, he passed relics of the earlier years of the conflict. There lay a water jug, twisted and maimed.

Slowly he crept forward to the line, alone with his thoughts. Would he be able to withstand the force of the other team's fire? Would his kneecaps take a hit? Would his shoes get dirty? Quickly he pushed these thoughts away and steadied himself. He bunched and sprang, leaping and running down the field. A hint of white and black caught his eye and reflexively he kicked. The soccer ball, old and deflated, flew true, sailing beyond the reach of the goalie, who popped out of the trench in front of the goal. The ball slammed into the upper corner, and the goalie sank to his knees, realizing it was over.

"Great job!" called the coach. "We're off to the Dome!"

Living for Soccer

CRAIG D. REID

My father came to both games. He rarely came to watch me play, but he was there, at the two games that meant so much to me. As I stepped onto the snow-covered pitch at that first one, nobody would ever have guessed that I was supposed to die from a terminal disease within five years.

I was a thin, short lad of 16, barely able to sprint ten yards before dropping from sheer exhaustion, but I could dribble a soccer ball. I could magically weave in and out between two or three players, within a three-yard radius, then pass the ball with pin-point accuracy, with either foot, up to fifty yards away.

I had learned to ignore my coach's chiding remarks that accused me of "dogging it" during practice and wing sprints. However, on game day, coach would always appreciate my control and finesse. "Fake 'em outta their jock straps," he used to say delicately.

I was naturally left-footed, but my father, a hard-nosed Scots professional player long before he brought us over to the States, used to force me to practice kicking with only my right boot on. My favored left foot was bare. Any attempt to kick the purposely water-logged ball with my left foot would have been not only foolish but painful. Although I played left wing, being able to kick with either foot always proved to be of great advantage, especially for kicking in-swinger corner kicks. Also, because of my lack of stamina and lung power, anticipation and field positioning had become my forte. I consistently played wide and timed my short runs into open spaces.

It wasn't so easy, coming from a soccer family of professional players and coaches, as I did. I didn't possess the blinding speed and tenacious vigor of my father or the physical power and endurance of my older brothers, though I did have patience and suppleness, I guess.

Only my family knew of my illness. Coaches, players and fans were all unaware of my internal pains and weaknesses, attributing my partly decrepit body to laziness and avoidance of weight training. On a good day, I could do three push-ups.

I imagine my father often wondered what it was like to play soccer with a debilitating lung disease. That's probably why he came so infrequently to my games. It probably pained him to see me with blocked sinuses, tight chest, pounding headaches caused by coughing so hard I couldn't inhale quickly enough to prepare for the next set of coughs. And all this compounded by frequent lapses of digestive failure. It must have hurt my father to see me struggle, always being knocked about, out-run and overpowered by crunching tackles. I would often return home with swollen ankles and badly bruised shins, but to me, these were the spoils of war that made me feel like a dangerous marked player.

Soccer was my niche, my escape from the constant reality that I had limited time to live. The idea of death had been with me for so long that I was immune to its fearsome face, but I was never prepared to accept the loss of my beloved sport. For ninety minutes at a time I could escape the ridicule of my classmates and forget their insults. I could rip apart an opponent's defense with just a few seconds of clean ball control, then follow with a "thread the needle" pass. Gone were feelings of inadequacy that I felt in trying to play football, basketball, and other sports.

One of my heroes was an English player named Sir Stanley Matthews, who played his last professional match when he was in his fifties. Matthews, one of England's greatest players, proved that size, speed and brawn were not always the key ingredients needed to be a successful team sport athlete. I embraced this ideal and hoped to be living proof of it.

*   *   *

The whistle blew. Soon into the game I was on the receiving end of a long through ball. I knew I couldn't outrun the speedy halfback, whom I saw out of the corner of my eye preparing for a slide tackle. I don't remember how I got to the ball and centered it. The halfback's ensuing header tallied the one-nil score as the barrage of cries from the fans showed their approval and satisfaction. Meanwhile, my overzealous play had instigated the familiar hacking cough attacks that I so feared. My face was a bright red from blood pumping furiously to my head by the irregular gagging coughing movements, and breathing convulsions consumed my body. The goal scorer was still receiving his accolades giving me more time to regain my composure before anyone else could see me struggling. It was a see-saw battle. The crowd was chanting and swaying back and forth reminiscent of an English F.A. Cup final in Wembley Stadium. But my father knew how much that goal had cost. The defender did, too, who helped me up and nodded to me as if he understood the difficulty I was having. I refused to quit.

And I didn't.

And then it happened—at the other game my father went to that I remember so well. It was my play of plays, the turning point in my life.

I trapped the ball and headed down the wing oblivious of the same pursuing defender I had outfoxed in the previous game. I dribbled with ease around four defenders, almost laughing as I did it. The field appeared to open up as the opponents seemed to back away. The goal mouth had grown to a whopping fifty feet wide by twenty feet tall. How could I miss this shot? My heart was pounding, the excitement was overwhelming, yet I felt no urge to cough and my head was clear.

This would have to be a right-footed shot. I was not intimidated. Thanks, Dad.

I started my kicking approach movement, the right leg cocked back like a whip ready to sting its opponent. It took supreme effort to dominate my excitement. This was it, my first goal of the season. My father would be proud . . .

There was a loud crunch as I hit the ground. I had been blind-sided by the pursuing defender. My body took off and landed about ten feet away from the point of impact. I heard the loud thud created by the collision, followed by an "oooh!" from the crowd. I lay on the ground, motionless, as the defender sneered at me and took the ball. I rolled over, opened my eyes and saw my father amidst the screaming crowd. I was hurt.

He made a gentle waving motion with his right fist. I focused. I could see he was saying something, but I couldn't make it out. I squinted and strained my eyes. I could now see the confident gleam in my father's eyes and his reassuring nod. The words were clear, "Get up, get up, get the ball, get the ball."

Nobody really understood what happened next, but in one swift motion I sprang to my feet and started to chase my assailant. I sprinted forty yards, and when I was five feet away from the defender I launched the best slide tackle I had ever done in my life. I must have slid at least ten feet before I stole back the ball from the now falling defender. I got up, passed the ball to the opposite wing, earning an assist. I didn't cheer for the goal, but instead turned around and helped up the fallen defender, hoping I had not hurt my older brother.

The whistle blew. The game had ended. But only the game. I never seemed to play soccer the same way afterwards. It was as if my old self had left and a new one seemed to get faster and stronger as the five years came and went. My love for soccer never faltered, and I didn't die.

Winning the game was not so important as being able to play it. Many with my disease seem simply to wait in their beds to die, while I was waiting on the soccer field to live. To this day, the coaches, players and fans don't know the full extent of what was going on during those games. To them, I was just another soccer player enjoying the game to the best of my ability, and that's the way it should be.

Hip Chargers:
How Women Impact the Game

RUTH CALLARD

No foul, No foul
"I got ball!" I howl
energy directed
I was elected
I charged her quite fairly
She landed quite squarely
I had the ball
But she got the call!
Tweeeeeeeet!
"The charge," said the ref, "must be with the shoulder . . . not the hip."

"Before play goes on" I pleaded
"Some clarification is needed."
"My hips are my weapon, not my shoulder"
I started to smolder
A tug on my shirt
My teammate did blurt
"Check out the rule book.
You know, those big guys built like inverted triangles. When they stand
    next to each other their shoulders touch."

This is a bit much
That rule book I had to see
There were no pictures of me!
I read a few lines
No hers and no she's!
I readdressed the referee
"But think of my anatomy
and my center of gravity
Hey ref I'm only five foot three!"

Biographical Notes

Ann Adams, Ph.D. in American literature, taught college courses in writing and literature for several years. She now homesteads in the Manzano Mountains of New Mexico, where she farms and writes.

B. W. Bales teaches literature at Carrizo Springs (Texas) Junior High School. Active on several soccer league boards, he has coached soccer at many levels in both Texas and Ohio and is the father of three soccer players.

Paul Bishop is a novelist and member of the Los Angeles Police Department in charge of sex crimes investigations, West Los Angeles area. He has played soccer in both the U.S. and England. Besides *Chapel of the Ravens*, he is the author of *Shroud of Vengeance*, *Citadel Run*, and *Sand Against the Tide*, as well as of numerous short stories.

Bryan J. Burkert is a former Atlantic Ten collegiate soccer player (St. Bonaventure University) and is now a business owner and freelance writer in Baltimore, Maryland.

Ruth Callard is Executive Director of the Women's Soccer Foundation in Seattle, Washington.

Doug Chapman covers soccer, tennis and hockey for the *Providence Journal-Bulletin*. He has played and coached tennis at the high school, college, and professional levels. He has a great affinity for English soccer and is a regular visitor to London.

116

Frank Dell'Apa currently covers soccer for the *Boston Globe* and the Portuguese language weekly, *O Jornal.* He began his career as a sports journalist at the *Nevada State Journal* and *Reno Evening Gazette* in 1972. He is co-founder and editor of *Alive and Kicking*, a soccer fanzine in Scituate, Massachusetts.

Sam Foulds, a retired engineer, has soccer roots that go back to junior high in 1918. He played for many years in Massachusetts and has been an officer in many New England and national soccer associations. He has written extensively on the game. In 1969, Foulds was elected to the U.S. Soccer Hall of Fame, of which he is a trustee. Associated with the U.S.S.F. since 1931, he was appointed historian of that organization in 1975.

Brendon Fowler, a student at Bowdoin College, played AYSO soccer for twelve years and was on JV and Varsity during high school in Clinton, New York.

Henry Gregory, a student at Brown University, has played soccer at all levels from house leagues to captain of the Brown Varsity team. Born in Birmingham, Michigan, he also lives part of the time in his father's native Greece.

S. S. Hanna teaches English at Geneva College in Beaver Falls, Pennsylvania (15010-3599). He is the author of *The Gypsy Scholar* (Iowa University Press) and has recently completed the manuscript of a book, *In the Days of Angi: Memoirs of a Writer Coaching Women*, from which "Birth of a Team" has been adapted.

Paul E. Harris, Jr. has been involved in soccer for most of his life. He played on championship teams in high school and college, has officiated more than 2,000 games, and authored twenty books on soccer, including *Fair or Foul*, a standard reference book for referees.

Jean Houston of Chapel Hill, North Carolina, is a soccer enthusiast, who loves "the right word, the right pass, and Dartmouth soccer," where her son Mike played. She works at the National Humanities Center.

Dick Johnson serves as Curator of The Sports Museum of New England in Cambridge, Massachusetts, where he has mounted exhibits celebrating such institutions as Fenway Park, The Boston Braves, and The Boston Bruins. He has co-authored the following books, *Ted Williams, A Portrait in Words and Pictures* with Glenn Stout and *Young At Heart, the Story of Johnny Kelley, Boston's Marathon Man* with Frederick Lewis.

Bill Littlefield is a commentator for WBUR in Boston and National Public Radio's "Morning Edition," where this piece originally aired. He teaches literature and writing courses at Curry College in Milton, Massachusetts. His most recent books are *Baseball Days* and *Champions: The Stories of Ten Remarkable Athletes*, both published by Little, Brown & Company.

Stuart Murray is an editor and writer as well as a former soccer player at Rutgers University (1965–1968) and with the German-American League and the American Soccer League (1967–1971). A native of Scotland, he has coached youth and high school soccer. Author of nine novels (eight under the pseudonym, Oliver Payne), Murray has also written four books of non-fiction, the most recent being *Norman Rockwell's "Four Freedoms"* for Berkshire House and *The Complete American Soccer Player* for Simon & Schuster.

Roscoe Nance, a sportswriter for almost two decades, has been covering soccer for *USA Today* for almost a third of his career. "Where have the years gone?" he asks. Gone to covering baseball, basketball, and football; and in soccer, gone to covering the qualifying games of the U.S. Olympic soccer teams of '88 and '92 and the '92 Olympic soccer matches in Spain. Nance also covered the 1991 FIFA Women's Championship in China, where the U.S. women were victorious.

Craig D. Reid, Ph.D., action fight choreographer and freelance writer in New Haven, Connecticut, was born with cystic fibrosis. Through soccer, martial arts, medications, and therapy, he lived beyond the life expectancy for victims of the genetic disease and in 1980 learned a breathing technique in Taiwan, which allowed him to give up all medications and traditional therapies. In 1986 he walked across America.

Diane M. Russwurm lives in Sayreville, New Jersey. When she is not being a soccer fan at her daughter's games, she is employed as a paraprofessional aide for the Old Bridge Township Public School system.

Philip J. Scrofani, Ph.D., is Director of Psychology for the Commission on Mental Health Services in Washington, D.C. and has a private practice as a clinical psychologist in Fort Washington, Maryland. Father of three soccer players, he has written a play on family issues for inner city youth and is completing a novel that projects the endangered status of the American family into the 21st century.

Nancy E. Seitz of Wayne, New Jersey, is one half of NanTuey, a writing partnership with Loretta B. Burdette of Atlanta, Georgia. Seitz is married to a former soccer coach and is mother of three one-time indoor-outdoor year-round soccer players.

Charles T. Shaw has been coaching and teaching at the Cranbrook Kingswood School in Bloomfield Hills, Michigan, since 1976. For twenty years he has been fighting to preserve from likely extinction the institution of the schoolmaster coach. "My small-town New Jersey soccer origins, which nostalgia has encased in amber," he writes, "enshrined the 2-3-5 system, each position having the distinctness and particularity of rooms in a museum."

David Updike is a teacher, writer, and photographer, who lives in Cambridge, Massachusetts. He has written five children's books and one collection of short stories, *Out on the Marsh*. He plays soccer for Diversity United, the over-30 champions of Rhode Island.

George Vecsey of the *New York Times* is among the few general sports columnists in the United States who would list soccer as one of their favorite sports. He has covered the World Cup in Spain (1982), Mexico (1986), and Italy (1990). He is the co-author of the autobiographies of Loretta Lynn, Barbara Mandrell, Martina Navratilova, and Bob Welch.

Fred L. Woodworth is a partner in the Detroit law firm of Dykema Gossett and heads the firm's Washington, D.C., office. He played on the Amherst College Varsity soccer team, 1959–1961. As President of the State Bar of Michigan, he wrote a monthly column for the *Michigan Bar Journal,* from which "*Ekecheiria* Revisited" has been adapted.